So. . . You Want to Build a House

So. . . You Want to Build a House

A Complete Workbook for Building Your Own Home

J. M. Gore

William Null

McGRAW-HILL

New York   Chicago   San Francisco   Lisbon   London
Madrid   Mexico City   Milan   New Delhi   San Juan
Seoul   Singapore   Sydney   Toronto

The **McGraw·Hill** Companies

Cataloging-in-Publication Data is on file with the Library of Congress

1 2 3 4 5 6 7 8 9 0   QPD/QPD   0 1 2 1 0 9 8 7 6

ISBN 0-07-147493-5

The sponsoring editor for this book was Cary Sullivan and the production
supervisor was Richard C. Ruzycka. It was set in Garamond by International
Typesetting and Composition. The art director for the cover was Handel Low.

Printed and bound by Quebecor/Dubuque.

McGraw-Hill books are available at special quantity discounts to use as pre-
miums and sales promotions, or for use in corporate training programs. For
more information, please write to the Director of Special Sales, McGraw-Hill
Professional, Two Penn Plaza, New York, NY 10121-2298. Or contact your local
bookstore.

This book is printed on acid-free paper.

Contents

About the Authors

J. M. GORE is a licensed real estate broker. She owns and operates her own real estate agency and construction firm.

WILLIAM NULL has owned and operated his own development and construction company and has worked as a construction superintendent for major homebuilders in the St. Louis, Missouri, area for more than 20 years. He has managed the construction of more than 50 homes at a time and has an impeccable record for finishing homes on time and on budget.

Introduction

If owning your own home is the "American Dream," perhaps then the pinnacle of the American Dream is to build your own house. A house tailored to not only fit your specific needs, but one personalized enough to make a statement to the world (or at least the neighborhood) of who you are. Customizing your special place and building it from the ground is a challenging, rewarding, and extremely fulfilling endeavor to undertake. Many people begin with tremendous plans and expectations only to get so burned by the building process that they determine to never build again. Our goal is to make this experience easier and even *enjoyable*.

Your home is usually the largest financial investment you will ever make. Therefore, you want to make quality decisions that add value to this investment, not useless and unnecessary costs. You want to stay within a budget and build the house in a timely manner.

Working for more than a decade with people who want to build a house, we recognize the mistakes and pitfalls commonly encountered by a would-be builder. The purpose of this book is to help you logistically and realistically plan and budget well before you begin, thus giving you a grasp of actual costs for construction and determining a reliable construction schedule to follow. By using this book, you will not only be better informed, but also be better prepared to handle the unexpected costs that arise so that your budget doesn't get out of control. You will also create a construction schedule so you can get an idea of when your project will be completed even when you encounter delays. Most people who want to build a house are shocked to discover the expense of all the things they want and need to include in the project. They get discouraged and confused before they even begin. This book will help you determine costs in advance so that you can make educated choices and control your budget. It will also help you avoid the worst feeling—to be near completion of your house and suddenly realize you are seriously over budget. You then hate the entire building experience and the house you have so diligently worked for.

This book is designed to help you accumulate all of the information you will need to successfully build a house with a budget you decide and design to fit your individual needs. The forms in the workbook section of this book will help you build an outline for the construction of your house. You will be able to navigate through the hard costs of construction, allowing you to choose the special things you want to be included in the house that will customize it to fit your needs, desires, and budget. You will learn to seek out the information you need to make informed decisions so that your house is not just a conglomeration of personal stuff, but a sound financial investment for your future. The building process is stressful. While no book can totally alleviate that stress, the intention of this book is to relieve a great deal of that stress by helping you compile information. Being informed, knowing what to ask, and whom to ask will resolve many of the issues that arise during the construction process. Good preparation will help you focus on the end result, allowing you to not only see the "big picture" but have control over your expenditures and budget. Knowing you are in control makes the undertaking of a large project less stressful, more rewarding, and fun. What seems like a daunting task at first becomes more like a challenge of a jigsaw puzzle when broken into smaller segments. By using this book as a useful tool, the construction of a new home will be a fun project.

As you discover how to determine the costs of each aspect in the building process, you will be in control and that will make this a rewarding experience. You may find that you enjoy this construction process. So, here's to building a great house!

Let's get started…

So. . . You Want to Build a House

1

The Startling Truth

THERE IS NO PERFECT HOUSE

It is one thing to want to build your dream house and to even get to the stage of building your dream house. You must realize from the very beginning that no matter what you, your architect or designer, and your builder do, and no matter how much money you have, there will be something unanticipated and the house will *not* be perfect. No matter how much you plan and prepare, the house cannot and will not be perfect. You will save yourself, your realtor, your architect or designer, and your builder unbelievable stress and discontent if you accept this truth before you even start. All houses differ from theory (the blueprint, specifications, and plans) to reality. No one can anticipate the unique situation of an individual house on a particular property. Even the subdivision house that is built over and over again has things happen that make it different each time it is built. Good carpenters and builders can cover up discrepancies and mistakes and that is what makes them skilled and good at their trade.

Understand the difference between a customized house and a custom house. A *customized house* can be a unique design that you, your designer, and builder have created; you are going to select items (perhaps even some custom-built items) to put into the house. A *custom house* is the one in which you personally hand select each piece of wood and everything else used to construct it. If you do not like a particular item or something about the house, you have the time and money to have it torn apart and reconstructed. Most people say they are having a custom house built, but mean they are having a customized house built. If you really are having a custom house built, you must tell your builder in advance because creating an accurate budget for a true custom house can be nearly impossible.

When building a customized house, you can make changes during the construction process. However, you must keep in mind that 99 percent of the time, if you make a change, you will be charged for it. This is true especially if anything has to be rebuilt or moved. Also keep in mind that some changes you desire may not be able to be made. Many times homeowners want to change walls and do not realize that a particular wall they want to move may be a load-bearing wall or it may affect an entire truss system or something else critical to the structural integrity of the house. Your builder should be experienced enough and honest enough to tell you when something is impossible or something that you will regret having done in the future. You must also be prepared to accept that even a seemingly minor change can affect the cost of numerous other items that no one can foresee when the changes are being made or considered.

Example: Once the framing began on a particular house, the homeowner wanted to change the dormers from nonworking dormers to working dormers that acted as skylights in each room. This entailed a little more labor for the framing crew and a little more 2 × 4 lumber and materials.

What was unforeseen: The drywall crew had to add a little more drywall and a great deal more labor because of the scaffolding now needed and the new degree of difficulty in hanging the drywall. The electrician then had to do additional wiring because electrical fixtures now had to be added. The electrical fixtures had to be special ordered because of the added 4 ft ceiling height in each dormer and the light fixtures chosen had bulbs that were very difficult to change. The windows became an issue because of their location, they were nearly impossible to clean and maintain. The homeowner ended up disliking the skylight effect that was created in the rooms involved, so special window treatments had to be purchased and installed.

Because of the location of the dormers, the window treatments had to have a remote control feature added. Decorating became very difficult because of the position of the dormers in each room since they were designed aesthetically to enhance the exterior of the house, not the interior. The total cost for the dormer change came to be $20,000. The homeowner was trying to create the perfect house and in the end hated that aspect of the house.

You will be much more successful and pleased with the end result if you do not try to build a perfect house. Instead, find a plan that meets your needs within your budget and add a few personal touches. You will end up with a more perfect house that will serve you well and resell well.

2

Purchasing the Property

It is better to purchase the property first and design the house to fit within the perimeters of the property lines and setbacks as well as any engineering requirements specified by the soil analysis of the property. When purchasing property as a possible building site, there are the questions you should ask the seller:

- **Is there a recorded plat and survey of the property?** If there is not, this is something you should have done before you buy the property. Usually this can be negotiated in the purchase price with the seller as to whether he or she will incur the entire cost, part of the cost, or none of the cost. It may be a good bargaining chip for you in making an offer. Get an estimate on either a full survey or a spot survey. Usually, if it is a small property or lot, a spot survey will suffice and may be only a few hundred dollars. If it is a larger piece of acreage, a full survey may cost thousands of dollars and take weeks to have done. There have been countless instances when a seller has sold a piece of property they thought they owned to a buyer who builds a house on it with no survey or plat. Much to the chagrin of both parties it is discovered at a later date that the seller was mistaken and did not own that particular piece of property, or that the property lines were not where everyone thought they were and the house is partially or totally on someone else's property.

- **Has the property been engineered or soil tested as a building site?** If the property is in a subdivision, the developer should have had an engineer do a soils analysis and compaction test to the specifications of the size and weight of homes he plans to build. He should be able to provide a letter from the engineering firms substantiating that the property you are buying will support the house you intend to build. Usually, in a subdivision, the developer will hire an engineer to test each lot to be sure that it will support the range of houses being built. An engineer will be able to tell you if the building site will be suitable for the particular house your want to build. If you are buying acreage, you should have the specific building site engineered for your particular house.

- **Be sure to ask about any fill areas in subdivisions or on acreage.** Many times developers have to fill areas or purchase properties that were used in the past as landfills. The developer should be willing to disclose if a particular lot has been filled and disclose the specific engineering on that lot. There have been numerous circumstances where a particular lot had a sinkhole or had been improperly filled. Also, the seller of any acreage should disclose if any part of the property has been used as a landfill or has buried tanks or trash on it. If a property has been improperly filled, once the weight of the house is on it, problems may begin to surface. Part of the house may settle twelve or more inches or may pull away from the rest of the house, requiring the entire house to be removed because of a sinkhole or other issue.

- **While asking about possible fill areas, also ask specifically about any hazardous waste dumps on any piece of property.** It is important to know if any area has *ever* been used as a tire, chemical, or any type of dump. Once an issue is discovered in a subdivision or on a particular piece of property, it may be too late to recoup your investment. If you ask the question in advance and the seller does not disclose this information, the seller is liable and the buyer has grounds for filing a lawsuit. However, keep in mind that once lawsuits begin being filed, the chance of recovery from the seller or a developer may diminish. Victory in such a suit does not ensure monetary recovery if the liable party does not have funds nor has funds shielded from such judgments.

- **Ask about any and all easements and rights-of-way.** When the title company does a title search, all easements and rights-of-way should be disclosed from a period of the past 25 to 50 years, but ask anyway. You must know about utility easements, what restrictions dictate, and exactly where you can build on a specific site. Many properties are virtually unbuildable because of size, setback restraints, and location of utility easements. You must know if you share any sewer and/or water rights or well easements on a property. If there are shared easements on a property, you must be advised of your responsibilities if repair work or maintenance is required. You must know about all road and access easements and what rights others have to cross and use your property as well as your responsibilities, liabilities, and limitations in this matter. If your property borders a landlocked property, it may be prone to a mandatory easement, thereby granting others access rights to the property.

Do not get discouraged. You do not have to be an engineer or lawyer to select the right piece of property, but you do need to ask questions about the property so that you can make an informed decision about the property.

3

Consult a Realtor

A good realtor can be a great asset in finding a building site, an architect, and a builder. Realtors are familiar with the area and should be able to assist in getting all the information you will need about the property. It is helpful to find a realtor who specializes in new developments or new construction. Realtors can advise you about the property values in an area and compile a comparable market analysis from their database about house values in different areas as well.

You should be candid with the realtor regarding your budget. If your budget is $250,000, a realtor can direct you to areas where you can get the most value in that price range as well as areas that have strong sales. Realtors are familiar with the more popular areas of growth in an area and where housing consistently appreciates well. Realtors can also advise you about different builders in the area and where to view their projects and workmanship.

Realtors can also tell you the important features of housing in your budget range. An example of this: In a particular area several years ago new houses priced from $215,000 and above were expected to feature jetted tubs in the master bath while homes less than that rarely had jetted tubs. Currently, homes priced in the mid-100s feature jetted tubs as common practice in many areas because of their popularity and lower cost.

If you are not purchasing or selling property through realtors and are just seeking advice and information, it is a common courtesy to periodically keep in touch and do business with them in the future if they were helpful.

4

Meeting with an Architect

If you are going to have a house designed, you should get acquainted with an architect or home designer as soon as possible. You may want to consult with the architect before you begin looking for property. He or she may be able to advise you of areas to look for property and know of subdivisions or acreage that will suit your requirements. If you are going to build a 3000 ft² sprawling ranch, the lot requirements may be quite different from building a 3000 ft² two-story house. The architect may be familiar with requirements for setbacks and utility easements in certain areas. The architect may also be familiar with county ordinances and permits required or can direct you in finding the information you will need. He or she will also be able to tell you if the plan must have an architectural seal for a project. This seal is usually reserved for commercial structures, but some circumstances or communities may require a seal for your house.

A good architect should be able to help with the budget to a certain extent. You need to tell him or her what your budget is in the very beginning. There is a great difference in creating floor plans and stylization between a $200,000 budget for a 3000 ft² house compared to a $300,000 or greater budget for a 3000 ft² house. Refer to Chap. 8 for detailed information. Discuss the use of a computer-aided design (CAD) drawing compared to a real blueprint with your architect. The CAD may be less expensive if making changes, but some CAD drawings lack structural details your builder may need.

When you hire an architect or a draftsman to design a house, the house plan becomes your property once it is paid for in full. He cannot share it with anyone else without your consent. If someone contacts the architect requesting a copy of your plans, the architect cannot give out a copy without your express written consent.

HOW MANY COPIES OF THE BLUEPRINT DO YOU NEED?

Plan on getting between 10 and 15 copies. Some will be lost, some destroyed, and some must be kept forever in a safe place. Here is the breakdown of who gets what, who will return them, and who will not.

If You Are Building with a Builder with His or Her Plans

- You will need one *working set* for yourself (you will have more). This set will be *your* master set to make notes on for any changes occurring during construction or problems.

Bank copy: The bank or lender will keep a copy on file.

- A copy should always remain with the home for any future owners (if you receive an *approved copy* from any municipality issuing permits, this is the best copy to keep for this purpose). Keep this copy in what will become your *permanent construction file*.

If You Are Building with a Builder with Your Plans

- You will need one *working set* for yourself (you will have more). This set will be *your* master set to make notes on for any changes occurring during construction or problems.

Bank copy: The bank or lender will keep a copy on file.

- A copy should always remain with the home for any future owners (if you receive an *approved copy* from any municipality issuing permits, this is the best copy to keep for this purpose). Keep this copy in what will become your *permanent construction file*.

- The builder or project manager will need a minimum of seven working sets of plans depending upon whether or not they will be getting bids for the construction.

- Each engineering firm hired will need a set of plans (soils analysis, septic, utility, and the like), and the plans may or may not be returned to you.

If You Are Getting All Bids Yourself

You will need all as listed above, but the seven or more master sets allotted to the builder will be what you will use for getting bids as follows:

- One complete set for lumber companies to bid from—this will be returned to you.

- One complete set for foundation and concrete crews and framing crew—keep this set in the house once the house is under roof for general reference by all crews. Be sure to transfer all notes and changes to this set from your personal master set.

- One partial set of front, back, and each side elevation for each masonry, siding, exterior cover, and roofing subcontractor.

- Four partial sets of entire floor plan without elevations for electrician, plumber, heating and air installer, insulation installer, cabinet company and designer, septic/sewer installer, drywallers, trim carpenters, and flooring company. These four sets can be rotated to each trade bidding the project. Tell each subcontractor who receives a set of plans that you will need the set for the next subcontractor to bid from and you will likely have the plans returned to you.

Be sure to ask how long it will take for the subcontractor or vendor to get the bid to you and how long they will need the blueprints. Depending on the size of the house and each subcontractor's work schedule, you may receive a bid in a few days or several weeks. Use the *blueprint log sheet* form (Fig. 4-1) in the Workbook section to keep track of who has which copy of the blueprint and how long they have had it so you know where the copies are at all times. When copies used for bidding are returned, keep them for each trade that will be doing the job. Any changes made on the master blueprint must be noted on all partial blueprints being used for bidding or construction purposes. Blueprints get destroyed and misplaced as a matter of course, but by keeping a log, you will be less likely to be caught without any sets over the course of construction.

BLUEPRINT LOG SHEET

Vendor or Subcontractor	Material or Trade	Phone Number	Blueprint Page	Date Out	Date Returned
MILLER COUNTY / JOHN	PERMIT	201 555-5512	1 SET		
CLEAR IT NOW / MARK	CLEARING	201 555-5512	PLAT	6/1	6/15
CLEAR IT NOW / MARK	EXCAVATION	201 555-5512	FOUNDATION	5/1	5/3
ABC ENGINEERING/JOE	SEPTIC ENGINEER	201 555-5512	PLAT & 1 SET	4/15	4/20
ABC CONCRETE / MIKE	FOUNDATION	201 555-5512	FOUNDATION	4/20	4/23
ABC CONCRETE / MIKE	FLATWORK	201 555-5512	PLAT/FNDTION	4/20	4/23
CUSTOM CONCRETE/JIM	FLATWORK	201 555-5512	PLAT/FNDTION	4/20	4/21
R & R LUMBER / GEORGE	LUMBER	201 555-5512	FLOORPLAN	4/1	4/10
R & R LUMBER / GEORGE	WINDOWS	201 555-5512	FLOORPLAN	4/1	4/10
ELLISON ROOFING / KEVIN	ROOFING	201 555-5512	1 SET	4/3	4/4
SPECIAL SIDINGS / LARRY	SIDING	201 555-5512	ELEVATIONS	4/5	4/7
BRICKS AND STONES/HAL	MASONRY	201 555-5512	ELEVATIONS	4/5	4/7
MHK CARPENTRY / MEL	FRAMING	201 555-5512	FLOORPLAN	4/3	4/4
MID-AM ELECTRIC / LEROY	ELECTRICAL	201 555-5512	ELECTRICAL	4/2	4/5
VITAL PLUMBING / JO	PLUMBING	201 555-5512	FLOORPLAN	4/2	4/5
FURNACE MASTERS / RON	HVAC	201 555-5512	FLOORPLAN	4/2	4/7
DELUXE CABINETS / BRIAN	CABINETS	201 555-5512	FLOORPLAN	4/10	4/13
JOE'S LANDSCAPES/ JOE	LANDSCAPE	201 555-5512	PLAT/FNDTION	4/15	4/20

SAMPLE

FIGURE 4-1
Blueprint log sheet.

5

Going to the Bank

If you approach the bank or lender with all of the preliminary information in this workbook in hand, they will know you are well prepared for the venture you are about to embark upon. Each lender handles new construction loans differently. You should contact several lenders in your area to see which one suits you best and which one meets your financing needs.

Some lenders will disburse the funds for construction loans in-house. You or the builder you choose will take the invoices to the lender. The lender will review the invoices, possibly inspect the property, and cut the checks to each subcontractor. The vendors or subcontractors will either pick up the checks directly from the lender and sign lien waivers at that time, or the checks will be given to you or the builder and it will be your responsibility to get the lien waivers signed when the checks are received. Most lenders require subcontractors to sign a lien waiver for each invoice issued to ensure they have been paid and that there are no outstanding invoices or possible liens against the property when construction is finished. If your lender disburses funds directly, you may save from 1 percent to 2 percent of *total construction cost* compared to disbursing through a title company. You will also have sizable savings because the interest charged during construction will be for smaller amounts throughout the entire construction period rather than four or five large draws during construction.

Disbursing through a title company is more costly, but the responsibility of getting signed lien waivers from each vendor and subcontractor is that of the title company. The lender or title company will advise you or your builder the allotted number of draws you are allowed to have during the entire construction period and the construction site will very likely be inspected before funds are disbursed. If your lender insists on using a title company, you need to ask how much the title company will charge and at what point they receive their payment.

In some instances, the fee a title company collects will be taken out of the construction loan immediately when the loan is first set up before construction is begun. Be sure to allow for this in your budget, as this can be a sizable amount of money that you were counting on for actual construction costs. Some title companies charge a percentage fee for each check they issue so their charges are spread over the entire construction period, and you would not be charged for anything you paid for with your own funds. This is better for you, so you are not paying interest during the entire course of construction for services that have not been totally rendered. You should also ask if there is an additional charge for any inspections the title company does, how many inspections they do, and if they inspect for each invoice presented and check written. Some title companies allow only five or six inspections during the course of construction and charge an additional $50 or $100 per inspection above your allotted amount. This can add thousands of dollars to your cost if construction goes slowly and more disbursements are needed because of delays.

You must also ask how long it takes for funds to be disbursed once invoices have been approved and turned in. Some title companies take weeks to process. This can create quite a problem for you in dealing with your vendors and subcontractors. Most subcontractors and vendors require at least a partial payment, if not the entire payment, upon delivery of goods or once their portion of the job is completed. Some require payment within five business days of services rendered. If your title company or lender is slow to pay, this can create quite a problem with having your vendors or subcontractors return to finish their respective jobs or deliver materials.

It is far better for the homeowner to be in total control of funds, disbursements, and lien waivers if you have the time to deal with it.

Remember that you are the customer and the title company you choose is up to you. Do some research and find one that is most efficient and fast with its services.

Figure 5-1 is a sample of a lien waiver form. Some lenders and title companies have their own forms. Originals are for the lender and/or title company. You should keep one copy for your files. If you have

WAIVER OF LIEN

SAMPLE

State of: ____Missouri_____

County of: ____Miller_____

Gladville, U.S.A. _____

To All Whom It May Concern:

Whereas, the undersigned has been employed by:

_____Mr. and Mrs. Happy Homebuilding Couple_____

to furnish labor and/or materials for the building known as:

LOT NUMBER: __123__ **SUBDIVISION:** _____Happy Acres_____

ADDRESS: _____456 Blissful Valley Avenue,_____

Now, therefore, the undersigned for and in consideration of the sum of ____Seven____

__Thousand Five Hundred and no/100__ ---------------------- **($7,500.00) dollars and other good and valuable considerations, the receipt whereof is hereby acknowledged, does hereby waive and release any and all lien, and claim or right to lien, on said above described building and real estate under the Statutes of the State of** ___Missouri___ **relating to Mechanic's Liens, on account of Labor or Materials, or both, heretofore furnished by the undersigned for said building and real estate.**

In the event the bank check given in payment of the foregoing materials and/or labor should be returned unpaid because of any fault or neglect of the make of the check, then this release shall become null and void.

Given under our hands this _____ day of _____, 20____.

By: _____
                    (Signature)

Title: _____

Company: _____

INVOICE NUMBER: _____   **CHECK NUMBER:** _____

FIGURE 5-1
Sample lien waiver.

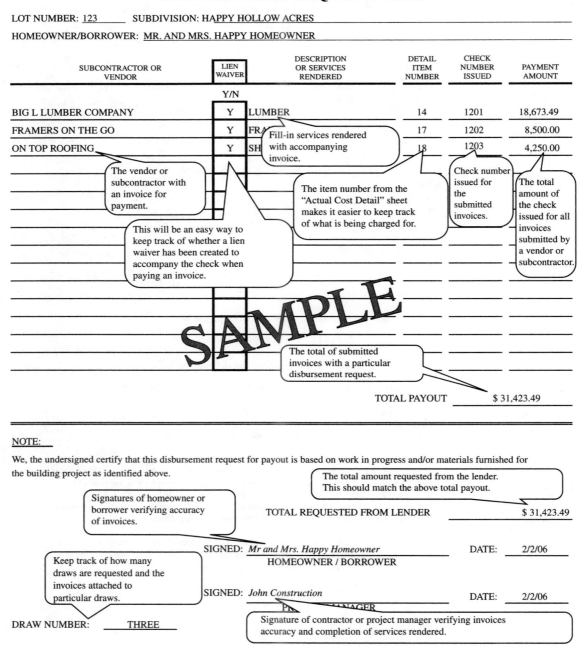

FIGURE 5-2
Sample disbursement request.

questions regarding lien waivers and their value, you should consult a real estate attorney in your area.

Figure 5-2 shows a sample of a *disbursement request* form which can be turned in to a lender or title company to request payment for invoices. You would fill out whom the invoice is from, if you have a lien waiver to give with the check to be issued, the description of materials supplied or services rendered, and the item number from the *actual cost detail form* (explained in Chap. 10). You would also record the check number issued for the invoice and the total payment amount. There may be circumstances when you will receive more than one invoice from a vendor and turn several in at one time, hence only one payment amount per vendor or subcontractor. The *total payout* area is the total of all payments for the particular disbursement and should be equal to the "total requested from lender" unless the homeowner is adding his or her own funds to the disbursement. The form will need to be signed by the homeowner and project supervisor indicating the work has been completed or materials ordered or received. The "draw number" area is to keep track of which invoices are being attached to a particular draw request. This is an easy way to organize and keep track of large amounts of money being paid for several services.

6

Guidelines for Building a Remarketable Home

Be honest and objective about the marketability of your home in the future. You may think that this is the last or only home you will ever live in, but 99 percent of the time it will not be, so you must choose wisely in all areas.

BUILD WITHIN THE GIVEN MARKET IN THE AREA

To put it simply, do not overbuild or underbuild the home in the area you choose. Building an expensive, luxury house in the country fifty miles from conveniences may be your absolute dream and desire. However, you must consider the consequences of doing this. If 95 percent of other houses in the area are valued at a fraction of the cost of the house you build, you will narrow your market to not only someone who has the means to purchase such a house, but also to someone with the same taste, style, and design as you. You may create a situation where you will either have the house on the market for a lengthy period of time or be forced to take well below not only market value but also what you have invested in order to find a potential buyer.

DOES THE HOUSE DESIGN FIT WELL WITH THE OTHER HOMES IN THE GENERAL AREA?

Of course, if you have the funds and whim, you can build any style of house anywhere you desire. Take into consideration the style of homes in the surrounding area, whether in a subdivision or a rural area. Most builders controlling the development of a subdivision will either approve the house plan you have submitted or a subdivision/ homeowner's association will approve the plan. In some circumstances, you will have the latitude to build whatever you want. While you want your house to be special and unique, you also want it to complement the area. Building a traditional Victorian style two-story house in a subdivision of contemporary ranches could be quite a mistake. While your house may be comparable cost wise, it may be very difficult to market to prospective buyers.

Generally speaking, home buyers who love a particular style of house will make their selections in subdivisions or areas where that particular style is prevalent. Also, having a very different style house in a subdivision may affect the sale of other houses in close proximity to that house. Not only may some potential buyers not care to own a Victorian-style two-story, but they may not want to look at it every day either.

An example of this happened in several subdivision developments during the seventies. Rustic-style houses were very popular with the dark colored brick and dark brown wood-trim exteriors. In two different subdivisions in two towns about 25 miles apart nearly all of the houses were dark brick rustic ranch style. In each subdivision, the planning committee approved the construction of very contemporary three-story Masonite-sided houses. While the homeowners of each of these houses loved what they had built, when the houses went on the market, it became very difficult to sell them. Each took several years to sell and many marketing tactics were used to try to sell the houses. Each house was painted several times trying to find the "magic" color to appeal to a buyer. Eventually each house did sell, but for more than $25,000 below the actual market value because of the unusual design for the area. The houses on either side of each of these houses also suffered in resale because they were next door to the *boxcar* houses.

DOES YOUR HOUSE FIT WITHIN THE PRICE RANGE OF THE HOUSES WITHIN AN AREA AND/OR SUBDIVISION?

Building the biggest and most expensive house on the block or even in a general area of houses does not mean that you will reap a bigger harvest when it comes time to sell; nor does building the smallest and least expensive in a subdivision or area. It is better to do a little research and try to be in a price range of 3 to 5 percent of the average priced house in an area.

Two cases in point:

1. A homeowner loved a particular subdivision where the low-end 1800 ft^2 houses appraised for $165,000 and the high-end 2200 ft^2 houses appraised for $185,000. The homeowner built a 4350 ft^2 house with numerous upgraded features including a $25,000 landscape package, ceramic tile flooring, and solid cherry wood cabinetry, which none of the other houses had. The construction cost was $350,000. Because of the appraised value of all of the other houses in the subdivision and general area, this house appraised for $275,000. Needless to say, neither the homeowner nor the lenders were happy that the house could not appraise for the construction cost not to mention the possibility of having any equity available.

2. Another homeowner loved a subdivision of houses ranging in size from 2600 to 3600 ft^2 and ranging in price from $185,000 to $220,000. The homeowner chose to build a 1650 ft^2 ranch in the midst of these much larger houses. His appraisal did not increase because of the other house values, but his real estate taxes increased because of the method used to calculate and add value to lower-end houses based on more valuable houses in the area. The homeowners' little house, although very nice, looked quite out of place compared to the others on the street.

When selling a house under the above circumstances, more is involved than just the aesthetic appeal of an area. The appraisal, or lack thereof, affects possible buyers who are seeking 80 percent to 90 percent financing.

RESEARCH THE GENERAL SQUARE FOOT PRICING OF NEWLY CONSTRUCTED HOUSES IN AN AREA

Markets vary greatly across the country. In some areas, a new house cannot even be constructed for $120/ft^2, while in other areas $120/ft^2

would be considered high-end. Seek out display houses in the area and calculate the selling square foot price for new construction. Be sure to take into consideration the variables that affect an area such as lake frontage, view, location, and so forth.

Most people today want more square footage for the money invested. The newer open floor plans can give one the feeling of greater space and still be economical. Contact local lenders and ask what the current square foot lending rate is for an area. For example, some lenders will lend at $75/ft^2$ for finished living space and $35/ft^2$ for unfinished storage space such as in a basement. This unfinished space may be converted to finished space in the future, adding great value to the home or greater marketability, because it can be priced lower with the possibility of increasing value by finishing the space in the future.

It is best to talk to lenders and even real estate agents in an area before getting started so you can begin with a realistic plan and budget.

LEARN THE VALUE OF AN UPGRADE

What will the added expense of an upgrade do for the value of the house? A prime example is insulation. In some areas, blown cellulose insulation is overall only a few hundred dollars more than bat insulation. The savings on energy bills throughout the lifetime of the house would be thousands of dollars. Therefore, the added value is great and a great sales point as well. This would be considered a value-added-cost because it pays for itself over the course of time and will always hold its value.

On the other hand, upgrading to custom cabinetry for a moderately priced house may not be the wisest of decisions. While aesthetically and emotionally satisfying to one individual, this item does not pay for itself and may not hold an intrinsic value to a potential buyer in the future.

7

Hard Costs versus Soft Costs

Dividing the cost of construction into hard costs and soft costs is very important when creating a budget.

Hard costs are the costs of whatever is *needed* structurally to construct the house. These items cannot be skimped on but can be added to in order to add more value or strength to a house.

HARD-COST ITEMS

- Excavation and clearing of property and backfill.

- Foundation—footings, wall structure, steel, drainage system, and waterproofing. Special effects, such as chipped or raked exposed walls, are extra.

- Concrete flatwork—usually basic driveway, patio, and sidewalk is concrete; however, extra wide, special effects and special materials and designs, such as exposed aggregate and stamped designs, are extra.

- Lumber, nails, adhesives, subflooring, and all framing materials needed for the basic structure.

- Windows—upgrading windows e-factor, styles of windows, casement windows versus carefree versus double-hung, and the like are upgrades to be considered, as well as whether windows are wood, vinyl clad, aluminum paned, and double or triple glass.

- Note: Tempered-glass windows are mandatory for all windows within 18 in of the floor and all sliding glass doors must be tempered glass. Also, consider adding the expense of shatter-resistant windows near the fairways of golf courses—this can become mandatory in certain circumstances.

- Insulation—consideration must be made whether the savings of using bat insulation outweigh the cost of blown cellulose insulation compared to future energy bill savings.

- Basic plumbing and electrical wiring (this is discussed in detail in the section "Soft Costs").

- Roofing materials—15 lb felt paper versus 30 lb felt paper must be considered as well as 3-tab asphalt shingles versus architectural shingles versus more expensive shingles. Check the roofing material warranty—some manufacturers sell the same product for 25- to 30-year shingles with the only difference being a longer paper warranty for 30-year shingles. The 40-year shingle adds considerable value to the cost ratio of a house, but in basic construction any roofing system beyond a 30-year architectural shingle would fall into the soft-cost category because of added material and labor expense.

- Exterior finish—exterior finish, while vital to the house, is considered in the soft-cost category because of the numerous products available.

- Drywall—basic drywall is a hard cost, but different texturizing methods and special corners such as bullnose as well as intricate designs become a soft cost.

- Painting—basic painting is a hard cost. The most practiced method today is to paint all walls in a house, including the ceiling, one basic color. Anything beyond the basic paint on the wall, such as some of the new paint techniques involving customization and a painter familiar with these applications and the time required to create them would be a soft cost.

- Millwork—a basic allotment must be calculated in the cost of a house and is considered a hard cost. Extra wide base, upgraded doors, and fancy moldings are a soft cost.

- Landscaping—a basic allotment for final grading, seeding a lawn, and planting a few shrubs is a hard cost. Intricate landscaping has become very popular and must be considered a soft cost.

- Construction cleanup—the fact of the matter is that the job site must be kept clean. Everyone including the subcontractors for each trade as well as the homeowner wants the job site to be clean; however, this is an area most seem to be reluctant to allot enough funds for. It is a hard cost although it fluctuates depending on how each subcontractor cleans up after himself and how much waste is generated throughout the project. It is important to remember that each trade should be given the common courtesy and professionalism to start their work on a clean job site. This allows the subcontractors to perform to the best of their ability, correctly and efficiently. A clean job site will save the homeowner, and the subcontractors, money as well.

SOFT COSTS

Soft costs are the demons. They are all the great things you want and even if you don't have the budget, you may go crazy and get them. They are a little bit here and a little bit there that add up to thousands of dollars when the last nail is hammered, the door is closed, and the house and its mortgage is yours. Some soft costs have a great value to cost ratio, but most of them are your great taste. The manager of a great cabinet store is perhaps the most honest of anyone when she tells potential customers, "You are already overbudget when you walk through that door." Be prepared to sacrifice some things in order to have others. It is the albatross of soft costs.

Soft-cost items include, but are not limited to

- Exterior finish—part of this involves the aesthetic and general look of the house. Some of it may be determined by subdivision restrictions and rules. Stone, masonry, exterior insulation and finish system (EIFS), and stucco products add a great deal of value as well as cost to the house, but these products usually outlast their initial cost, so the cost-to-value ratio is good. Siding can be a less expensive alternative, but be advised that cheap siding will look cheap just a few months after it is installed. Choosing an exterior siding product that requires maintenance and/or painting may affect the marketability of the house in the future. The rule-of-thumb is to spend as much as the budget will allow for the exterior of the house, but be sure to keep it within the realm of the other houses in the area. Although a brick and stone house has tremendous value, in a subdivision of all vinyl-sided houses, it may not be able to bring its full price potential.

- Plumbing fixtures—talk to your plumber. A plumber will tell you what is popular and will last longer. Choose your finish wisely and stay consistent in each room (don't mix brass faucets with chrome door hinges). Be sure your house warrants very expensive fixtures because plumbing fixtures add little to an appraisal; but also know that cheap plumbing fixtures not only do not last, but are also easy for a potential homebuyer to spot as a negative about a house.

- Electrical fixtures—the rule-of-thumb is to choose more expensive fixtures in rooms that are used the most. Do not skimp on the exterior fixtures as they will show wear and tear first.

- Cabinetry—the number one place to go way overbudget. Good cabinets are nice, and great cabinets are great, but do not necessarily add a good value compared to cost ratio. Be sure to consider the structure of the box rather than just the door design. An expensive, poorly constructed cabinet is worthless and will fall apart in short order during normal living conditions.

- Millwork and trim—standard is $3^1/_2$-in base and 3-in door casing. If you choose a base that is more than $4^1/_4$ in wide, you must be sure to tell the workers who are doing the ductwork, so they install the cold air returns and registers at the right height. The most expensive, solid wood doors may not always be the most desirable if you live in a high-humidity area because the doors will swell. Be sure to ask before you buy.

- Floor coverings—there is no wrong answer because they can be replaced and give your house a facelift a few years down the road. Floor coverings is the area that is usually the one where the axe falls when cutting the budget because of the ease of replacing less expensive materials in the future with something more desirable.

- The above items are discussed in more detail in Chap. 8.

8

Learning to Spread Your Budget over the Cost of the House

The key to spending wisely and getting the most into and out of your house is in learning how to spread your budget as evenly as possible over the entire expenditure of the house while also allowing you to have those things you really want. The rule: *Do not overspend in any one given area.* Repeat. *Do not overspend in any one given area.* Every potential homeowner who is planning on building has an idea of what his or her budget is. It is unfair and even unethical to approach a builder, realtor, or lender and not be totally candid about this because everyone will most certainly know what the budget really is when the construction is complete.

Your responsibility is to determine how to divide your available funds to best serve you and give you the most value for your investment. You must either begin with the land you like or the plan you like. This is even the case if you are choosing one of several floor plans in a subdivision. Choose the land or choose the plan. If you are lucky, your favorite land and plan will be meant for each other.

LAND

Whether it is a lot in a subdivision or just a vacant land, you must decide what you are going to spend for and find its true value. You will pay more for a developed piece of property. However, the savings incurred by not having to deal with the expenses and issues associated with running utilities as well as the difficulties associated with developing raw land are usually well worth the cost of a developed site. Most lenders want the cost of the constructed improvement to be a minimum of $2\frac{1}{2}$ to 3 times the cost of the property. Therefore, if you spend $100,000 on the parcel of property, the cost of the construction of the house should be close to $300,000. This is the best utilization of the cost-to-value ratio of the land. Building a $100,000 house on such a property would not increase the ultimate value of the property and may actually decrease its value and that of surrounding property.

Consider the property and how excavatable it is. If it is a sheer cliff, is it practical to build on it? What is the composition of the soil? Is it dirt, rock, or sand? Are there numerous trees and how big are they? How much money will have to be allotted for land clearing? Can the brush be burned or must it be hauled away? Will the excavation costs so exceed the cost/value of the house that it will be impossible to build a house worth the excavation costs? Can the property be excavated and is there a local subcontractor with the skill to do it? If the property has a great deal of rock, can the cost of excavation be determined prior to the work being done, or will it be a time/equipment cost? What type of equipment will be needed for excavation and is it available in the area? Will the cost of excavation deplete your budget too much to substantiate the cost of the balance of the house? An experienced builder, developer, or excavator can answer these questions, and many more that may arise.

UTILITIES

Are the utilities already on the property? If not, you must determine this aspect of developing the land and budget for it. If the property already has all or some of the utilities, you must know what the various costs are to tap into the existing system and if you are allowed to tap into the system. In some circumstances, the utilities may have been run in an area, but the cost to tap on is so extreme that there is no benefit to do so.

Example: A developer paid to run the electric, water, and natural gas lines to a subdivision he was developing. The cost of this was defrayed into each of the lots of the property the developer owned. The properties that bordered his property could now have access to utilities that were previously not available, such as natural gas; however, in order to tap into this new system, each property owner had to reimburse the developer for his expense to run the utility to that point. The property owners also had to pay to run the gas line from their houses to the junction in the street. The initial cost of this for the property owner was in excess of $25,000. It was more economical for the property owner to keep a propane tank.

LAY OF THE LAND

How does the lay of the land affect the design of the house? Will there be a full basement, partial basement, crawl space, slab, or combination of these things? If there is a basement, will it be a walk-out or in-ground? Is it customary for the basement to have insulated walls in the area where the house is being built? How does the lay of the land determine the height of the basement walls? What is the trend in the area for the wall height? Eight-foot basement walls were common until more recent designs incorporated nine-foot and greater basement walls. Lots with a steep terrain can allow the concrete walls to be bench-stepped so that most of the wall is framed, which saves a great deal in foundation expense. Depending upon the area, concrete can be more expensive for materials and labor compared to lumber, framing, siding, and interior finishing, so this can be a huge budget factor. Will the elevation of the lot increase the labor cost because of degree of difficulty and/or special equipment needed for excavation or construction? Will the location of the property add costs to the project because of delivery fees? Over the course of construction, additional fees can add thousands of unanticipated dollars to the cost of a project.

HOUSE DESIGN

When approaching an architect, draftsperson, or builder, you should be honest about your budget. These people are professional and if you are not honest about how much money you really have and want to spend, they cannot serve you well. Most designers or builders will know immediately if your budget is realistic as soon as you start telling them what you want and how much you plan to spend. It is unfair and unrealistic to approach a builder and ask, "How much does it cost per square foot to build a house?" It is one thing to ask a lender what they lend per square foot for general residential construction, but the builder needs information. A good analogy would be to ask someone how much it costs to go to a grocery store and fill a cart with products. There is no way to give a price without having the information of all the contents of the cart. The builder must know everything about the house you want in order to give a fair price and help with your budgetary needs.

As discussed in the previous chapter, in general hard costs will change very little while soft costs are more variable and controllable. Keep in mind when designing a house or choosing a floor plan that the following items add to the overall cost of construction:

- **Roof pitch and number of gables as well as roof design.** The steeper the pitch of the roof is and the more gables the roof has makes the house more expensive. A hip roof is much more expensive than a simple gable roof.

- **Offsets and corners throughout the house.** In general, every corner adds $2000 to the cost of construction. This amount varies depending upon the exterior materials used.

- **Location of plumbing throughout the house.** The more centrally located bathrooms and kitchens are to each other, the more economical plumbing costs will be. Also keep in mind that all plumbing walls should be built with 2 × 6 studs rather than 2 × 4 studs. This makes the plumbing runs easier on the plumber and allows for additional needed insulation on exterior walls.

- **Special electrical wiring.** Television, cable, phone jack outlets, recessed can lighting, indirect lighting above or below cabinets, and lighting offsets in ceiling coffers, as well as wiring for complicated audio and entertainment systems add to the cost of construction very quickly.

- **Octagon or odd-shaped rooms and bay windows.** These items add extra cost for trusses, lumber, roofing material, labor, windows, flooring, drywall, and the like.

- **Decks and patios.** When considering wood decks, take into account not only materials and labor for construction, but also annual maintenance for waterproofing and staining.

- **House setbacks.** The setback of the house from the street affects utility runs, concrete for driveway, and landscape costs.

- **Vaulted ceilings and ceiling heights.** Vaulted ceilings add cost for trusses, drywall, painting, and ceiling fixtures. General ceiling height adds cost in framing, lumber, drywall, painting, and ceiling fixtures.

- **Windows.** The number, shape, size, and quality of windows must be carefully considered in the budget. Of course, if one of the property features is a great view, the value of numerous windows will offset the cost.

These are all items that add some value to the house depending on qualities of the building site, but you must determine if the item is a cost or value to the overall of the house.

Once you settle on a house design, you are able to calculate the hard costs to build the house. The soft costs are where most people get into trouble with their budget as they have a million-dollar taste and a minimal budget. The soft costs are where you, the homeowner, have the most control and must decide where to go overbudget a little or where to cut back a little in order to add something special and unique to the house. This is where your time is well spent doing as much homework as possible and familiarizing yourself with the costs and values of things like lighting fixtures, plumbing fixtures, cabinetry, and so on.

BASIC CONSIDERATIONS

- **Plumbing fixtures.** It is better to choose a high-quality standard fixture than a cheaper, fancier version. Beware of plumbing fixtures with plastic parts as they do not stand up to the normal wear and tear of use. Also, most plumbers will *not* warrant either fixtures they do not supply or that have plastic interior parts. If you do not have the budget for an upgraded fixture supplied by the plumber, do not waste your money on the "cheap" upgrade because it will cost you more in the long run. Choose your fixtures before construction begins and tell your builder what fixtures you have chosen. Many of the upgraded fixtures must have certain parts installed during the rough-in phase of plumbing or special framing may be required. Also, keep some consistency throughout the house with fixtures chosen. Every bathroom does not have to be the same style or finish, but mixing chrome and antique bronze in a room usually doesn't work well. One particular room may warrant a nice upgrade such as the kitchen or master bath. A house valued at $250,000 or less does not necessarily warrant upgrading a powder room with a freestanding sink with an in-wall faucet fixture priced at more than $3000, whereas a house valued in the $800,000 range may require this type of upgrade. Will a future buyer realize the value of a $1200 stainless sink over a $200 one? Does the house warrant marble tubs and showers in every bathroom, or just the master bath? Did the builder cut costs by installing acrylic tubs and showers instead of marble in a high-end house where all marble is expected? Is it obvious that one area or feature of the house has been overspent on and looks out of place?

- **Electrical fixtures.** Electrical fixtures can be chosen once construction has begun, but as always, it is better to select early if there is going to be a special fixture or lighting feature and advise the builder of this. The framing crew and electrician will need to know if anything has to be added structurally or wired specially for the fixture. It is better to begin with a basic budget of $1000 per $100,000 cost of house and add to or subtract according to the budget. This gives you a starting point. Be advised that you will probably go overbudget in this area, but how much is up to you. Break your budget down into specific rooms and try to be equally extravagant or frugal in each room. If you are going to be lavish with plumbing fixtures in the master bath, don't install a $15 light fixture because it will be obvious that the lights received the budget axe. Rule-of-thumb is if you upgrade the plumbing fixtures, upgrade the light fixtures, flooring, and towel bars as well. Even an untrained eye can tell that a bathroom with a marble, jetted-tub, cheap plumbing fixtures, expensive lighting fixtures, and plastic towel bars does not look right. Keep a room consistent.

- **Cabinetry.** Variety is as vast as the taste of each individual. If you decide that you must have the $35,000 solid cherry-wood cabinets, realize that a future potential homebuyer may not have the same value system and may not think the price of the house warrants such an expensive item. Expensive cabinetry does not necessarily add as much value to an appraisal as other items and one must realize that the cost of expensive cabinets may be only for the pleasure of the individual. Be sure to talk to the cabinet sales person about features that are important to you and find out if some things like inset doors are practical in your area. Sometimes high-humidity conditions in an area cause wood to expand, which affects the ability of the doors to close properly.

- **Countertops.** Be wise about the countertop material you choose. The new granite and solid surface materials are wonderful, but can be 6 to 7 times more expensive than laminate tops. With some of the newer laminate finishes that look like granite, you may be able to have the look without the added expense. If you do decide on an expensive countertop surface, be sure to upgrade the cabinets to properly complement the tops. Even an inexperienced person can see the mismatch of an expensive countertop installed on a cheap cabinet. Also keep in mind that the cheap cabinet will not last as long as the expensive countertop and may need to be replaced before the countertop. Also keep in mind that if you plan to live in the house for more than 5 years, you may enjoy giving the house a "facelift" with new cabinetry in the future. Don't forget to allow for the cabinet knobs and pulls in the budget. This is a commonly forgotten or underbudgeted area. Knobs can range in price from about $1 to well over $100 each. If you consider that you may have 30 to 60 or more knobs to purchase, the cost adds up quickly.

- **Flooring.** There is an abundant selection to choose from. Flooring is an area where you can cut costs, if you think that several years in the future it may be something you want to replace. It is easy to replace vinyl linoleum and carpet which can be the least expensive products to choose. Ceramic tile and hardwood products that last longer are more difficult to replace and cost more. There are less expensive ceramic tiles available, but keep in mind that they do not stand up to the abuse more expensive tiles can withstand. Upgrading flooring with tile and hardwood does help increase the appraisal value of the house, but choosing too expensive a product may not add enough value if the majority of the houses in your area have the less expensive floor coverings. If you have small children, you may want to consider choosing a less expensive grade of carpet and plan to replace it in a few years when there is less abusive traffic on it. Also consider that you may be ready for your house to undergo a change or renewal in a few years because you will become bored with your original selections and will want to keep with new trends.

- **Millwork and trim.** This is an area where extra expense can add up quickly. When selecting trim, common base is $3^1/_2$ in, door casements are 3 in, and most interior doors are split-jamb and prehung. Usually, trim throughout the house is painted white or stained, although with the correct decorating theme, trim can be painted using a contrasting color in one or all rooms. Upgrading to prefinished base and doors may save enough in paint and labor to justify the added cost. Keep in mind that by upgrading to a wider base you should also upgrade the door casements to a wider and matching base. Once the decision has been made to change to the wider casements, the split-jamb doors with casing must be changed to flat-jamb doors without casing and the door casing will have to be custom-cut which will increase trim carpentry labor costs. This must be discussed in advance with the trim carpenter as this will affect his or her charges greatly.

Example: A trim carpenter had been given a blueprint and bid the trim-out of a house based on installing split-jamb doors with casements and running $3^1/_2$-in base. He bid the job before the house was started. When the homeowners went to select the style of interior door for the house, they decided to buy $5^1/_4$-in fancy base and matching casing all unfinished so that they could have it custom stained. They were shocked to find that the trim carpenter was going to charge hundreds of dollars more. He now had to custom-cut the door casements for 29 doors (times two sides is 58 door casements). He also had to do more tedious work to properly install the fancy, wider base because he had to custom-cut around cold air returns, and several windows that were close to the floor. He did do the job, but what had originally been projected as a five-day job turned into a three-and-a-half-week job.

The reason for this chapter has been to enlighten you and try to make you look at the broader picture. You must be as objective as possible and try to see how your selections will add value or cost to your house and whether those choices will be profitable or costly to you in the long run and in the resale value of your house. By spreading the costs evenly throughout your house, you will have a house that should appreciate well in the real estate market. By limiting the upgrades in one or two rooms, you will be able to stay within your budget while enjoying your home as long as you are there.

9

Getting the Estimates

O nce you have purchased the property and the house plan is finalized, it is time to compile the costs and the estimates. This can be fun, scary, and dreadful. If you have chosen a builder, he or she will do or have done all of this for you. Builders have different methods of estimating the cost of a house and how they will charge for their services.

Most builders build a turnkey house. They mark up the costs for all labor and materials and this is how they make their profit. In this circumstance, the more upgrades you choose, the more profit the builder makes. Usually, this type of builder may also be the developer of a subdivision, so you will have several house plans and layouts to choose from and different customizations you choose will add specific costs to a house. Once construction begins, if you decide you want to make a change, you will be required to sign a *change-order form*. This form is in essence an amendment to the contract you have with the builder, and you will be responsible for the additional expense of this change. In some circumstances, you will also be charged a penalty fee for making the change after construction has begun. The penalty fee may be as little as $50 and can be as much as several hundred dollars and is usually payable in advance when you sign the change-order form. If your change is something the builder feels is very personal or customized, he or she may ask for the entire cost of the change to be paid for in advance and stipulate that this charge is nonrefundable should you back out of the contract or decide not to close on the house. The builder may demand this for something that seems small to the homeowner like the color of the wall paint or a siding color because he or she may feel this could affect the resale of this house or other houses in his development. This is the way a builder can better control his or her project and construction schedule, because changes cost everyone a great deal of time and money. Something that takes 2 days to change may affect the entire construction on a house by weeks because of the scheduling of crews and materials to compensate. Builders try to discourage changes because they are costly to everyone. The best thing to do is decide on what you want your house to be like before construction begins.

Some builders will get bids from all of the vendors and subcontractors on a house and charge you for the specific services they render (i.e., any labor they furnish, construction supervision, construction clean-up, etc.). This can save you a substantial amount of money since builders' markups may range anywhere from 10 percent to as much as 100 percent on certain items. Most builders will make somewhere between 10 percent and 25 percent on a project over and above the cost of materials and labor. A builder may or may not disclose his or her costs to the homeowner. This is considered privileged information and most suppliers and vendors will not disclose the builders' cost of materials. A builder developing a subdivision is less apt to reveal any cost information to the homeowner.

If you are having a house built on your own property by a builder, you should ask the builder for an itemized detail of all costs associated with the construction of your house. The builder will have to supply lien waivers for all materials and labor and the amount paid will be on the lien waiver form. Before construction begins, you should get estimates of all costs and fill out the comparative cost estimates, electrical fixture worksheet, and preliminary construction estimates worksheets. This may seem cumbersome, but this is your foundation for creating a real budget for your construction project. If the builder has compiled all of the estimates, this will be an easy task. Once you are able to compare prices and what you get for the expense, you will be able to make wise decisions about where some things need to be decreased or increased. This will also give you the basis of where every penny of your construction is spent.

Whether you are using a builder/developer of a specific subdivision or using a builder for your own property, be sure to ask if and what you will be charged for any upgrades. There have been circumstances of homeowners upgrading what they thought would be a few hundred dollars and find that they were charged many hundreds more because of change-order penalties, restocking charges, and builders' markup.

Example: The homeowners decided they would upgrade the refrigerator from the $900 standard model in the original bid to the $1700 model. They expected the $800 additional charge; however, when they went to the closing the charge was $3400. They were charged a change penalty, a 25 percent restocking fee for the refrigerator they did not buy, and the builder's 100 percent markup. Because of their contract with the builder, they had to pay. Please be aware that it is very common for all vendors to charge a 25 percent or greater restocking fee for any item that has been ordered.

It is recommended that you take the time and energy to get the cost estimates from several suppliers and subcontractors yourself. This is not to suggest that once you start working with a builder and he has put forth the time and effort to get estimates for you that you change midstream to another builder. If you find his or her ethics or quality of work lacking, then a change is deemed necessary. If you get some of the estimates, you will have better knowledge of comparison, but be sure the things you are getting estimates on are comparable. If you are getting a lumber bid from several suppliers, be sure not to just look at the bottom line, but at the quantities also. Lumber companies are notorious for shorting amounts needed to make the estimate appear lower; then when the actual construction is underway you may find that a much greater quantity of materials is needed.

10

How to Use the Workbook

The sample forms given in this chapter have been created to help you get started for actually using the homeowner's construction workbook.

The *comparative cost estimates* form is broken down into two categories.

Cabinetry is designed to allow you to compare the costs of four different brands and styles of cabinetry for your house. Usually one brand and/or color and style will be used throughout the house, but you are not limited to this tradition. It is becoming more common to mix and match brands and colors in kitchens and master bathrooms. This form allows you to break down the individual kitchen cabinetry cost, master bathroom cost, three additional bathrooms, laundry room cost, and two miscellaneous extra costs (perhaps for garage or basement). By breaking down each group into its cost, you will be able to compare and decide which provides the best value to you for the cost of the product. An area is provided for you to make notes about products, styles, and suppliers.

Plumbing, like cabinetry, is also divided into kitchen, master bathroom, three additional bathrooms, laundry room, and two extra areas for special needs (Fig. 10-1).

COMPARITIVE COST ESTIMATES

CABINETRY:

CABINET BRAND / STYLE	KITCHEN COST	MASTER BATH ROOM COST	BATH #1 COST	BATH #2 COST	BATH #3 COST	LAUNDRY COST	EXTRA	EXTRA	TOTAL
AB Bradn/Maple Cathedral	9,565.00	1,575.00	950.00	425.00		591.00			$ 13,106.00
Kitchens Plus / Oak Raised	7,250.00	1,720.00	850.00	523.00		508.00			$ 10,851.00
Classic / White Raised	8,375.00	1,775.00	625.00	502.00		617.00			$ 11,894.00

NOTES:

Linked the maple finish and color best - better hardware and drawers, but more than budgeted.

PLUMBING FIXTURES:

FIXTURE BRAND / STYLE	KITCHEN COST	MASTER BATH ROOM COST	BATH #1 COST	BATH #2 COST	BATH #3 COST	LAUNDRY COST	EXTRA	EXTRA	TOTAL
Alpha / Antiquity Chrome	354.00	754.00	640.00			235.00			$ 1,983.00
Foster/Modern Brushed Nic	653.00	985.00	678.00			350.00			$ 2,666.00
Metaquatic/Contemp/Brass	795.00	894.00	763.00			363.00			$ 2,815.00

NOTES:

FIGURE 10-1
Comparative cost estimates.

SAMPLE PRELIMINARY CONSTRUCTION ESTIMATES WORKSHEETS

These worksheets allow for the comparisons of two bids in every category of construction. If you get more than two bids or estimates, you need to narrow the possibilities to two bids and record their estimate amounts in the respective columns. By keeping track of these, you will be able to make decisions regarding what you are willing to allow for the budget in certain categories. You may not always take the lowest price if the vendor or subcontractor offers a better value for the cost of the service or product. This will also allow you to compare the price of your top two choices in each category (Fig. 10-2).

CONSTRUCTION ESTIMATES WORKSHEET

LOT NUMBER: 123   **SUBDIVISION:**   Happy Acres

HOMEOWNER: Mr. and Mrs. Happy Homeowner

	Item or Description	Vendor / Subcontractor	Amount of Estimate Number 1	Amount of Estimate Number 2
1	ALL PERMIT FEES			
2	ALL UTILITY TAP FEES			
3	BLUEPRINTS / DRAFTING / COPIES			
4	CLEARING	Dig and clear	1,500.00	1,350.00
		Big Boy Excavating		
5	EXCAVATING AND ROUGH GRADING	Dig and clear	2,500.00	3,500.00
		Big Boy Excavating		
6	BACKFILL AND FINAL GRADE	Dig and clear	1,200.00	1,100.00
		Big Boy Excavating		
7	UTILITY INSTALLATION	Water In The Ground	2,200.00	3,250.00
		Greens Utilities		
8	FOUNDATION	ABC Concrete	13,000.00	17,000.00
		Joe's Concrete		
9	FLATWORK	ABC Concrete	7,800.00	7,500.00
		Joe's Concrete		
10	WATERPROOFING AND DRAINTILE			
11	MASONRY			
12	SEPTIC / SEWER SYSTEM			
13	STEEL AND IRON			
14	LUMBER			
15	CARPENTRY FRAMING LABOR			
16	DECK MATERIAL AND LABOR			
17	TRUSSES AND CRANE TO SET TRUSSES			
		SUBTOTALS		

FIGURE 10-2
Preliminary construction estimates worksheet.

SAMPLE ITEMIZED COST DETAIL FORM

Once you have decided upon the vendors and subcontractors who will do your work and have accrued all costs for permits, tap fees, and so on, you will be ready to create a detailed cost of each item needed for the construction of your house. As bills and invoices are paid, insert the amount of each item in the "amount" column and

ITEMIZED COST DETAIL FORM

PERMIT FEES:	AMOUNT	SUBTOTALS
SUBDIVISION		
COUNTY BUILDING	125.00	125.00
CITY BUILDING		
FIRE INSPECTION		-
WATER		-
SEWER / SEPTIC		-
TERMITE INSPECTION		-
GAS		-
PHONE		-
CABLE		-
ROAD / STREET		-
ELECTRIC TAP FEE:	225.00	350.00
ADDITIONAL:		
		-
		-
TOTAL	$ 350.00	

BLUEPRINTS:	AMOUNT	SUBTOTALS
COPIES	235.00	
CHANGES		235.00
ORIGINAL DESIGN LAYOUT	2,000.00	2,235.00
		-
		-
		-
TOTAL	$ 2,235.00	

SURVEY AND LAYOUT:	AMOUNT	SUBTOTALS
SURVEY	375.00	
LAYOUT	125.00	500.00
		-
		-
		-
TOTAL	$ 500.00	

FIGURE 10-3
Sample itemized cost-detail form.

keep a running subtotal in the "subtotals" column. At the end of each category, carry down the last subtotal number to the bottom of the amount column for a total for that category, once all invoices have been received and paid. Once a category is completed the total cost is entered and the amount will be transferred to the *cost detail form* in the next section (Fig. 10-3).

ITEMIZED COST DETAIL FORM

CLEARING/EXCAVATING:	AMOUNT	SUBTOTALS
CLEARING	3,500.00	
ROUGH EXCAVATION	8,250.00	11,750.00
ROUGH GRADING	1,200.00	12,950.00
BACKFILL	3,200.00	16,150.00
DIRT REMOVAL / ADD	1,000.00	17,150.00
FINAL GRADING	1,350.00	18,500.00
		-
		-
		-
		-
		-
TOTAL	$ 18,500.00	

FOOTINGS AND FOUNDATION:	AMOUNT	SUBTOTALS
FOOTINGS	1,500.00	
FOUNDATION WALLS	9,000.00	10,500.00
RETAINER WALLS		
PIER PADS	1,000.00	1,000.00
ROCK	500.00	1,500.00
		-
		-
		-
		-
		-
		-
TOTAL	$ 12,000.00	

UTILITY INSTALLATION:	AMOUNT	SUBTOTALS
ELECTRIC FROM HOUSE	500.00	
GAS FROM HOUSE		
SEWER LINE FROM HOUSE	1,500.00	1,500.00
WATER FROM HOUSE TO METER	150.00	1,650.00
WATER FROM METER TO MAIN	150.00	1,800.00
		-
		-
TOTAL	$ 2,300.00	

FIGURE 10-3
(*Continued*)

ITEMIZED COST DETAIL FORM

DRIVEWAY AND FLATWORK:	AMOUNT	SUBTOTALS
GARAGE FLOOR	1,500.00	
BASEMENT FLOOR	1,500.00	3,000.00
DRIVEWAY	3,500.00	6,500.00
PATIO PAD	500.00	7,000.00
SIDEWALK	500.00	7,500.00
		-
		-
		-
		-
		-
		-
TOTAL	$ 7,500.00	

SEPTIC / SEWER INSTALLATION:	AMOUNT	SUBTOTALS
SOILS ANALYSIS	300.00	
SEPTIC ENGINEERING	900.00	1,200.00
SEPTIC EXCAVATION	900.00	2,100.00
SEPTIC INSTALLATION	4,000.00	6,100.00
ELECTRIC TO PUMP METER BOX	400.00	6,500.00
		-
		-
		-
TOTAL	$ 6,500.00	

WATERPROOFING / DRAINTILE:	AMOUNT	SUBTOTALS
DRAINTILE MATERIAL	195.00	
DRAIN PIPE AROUND FOUNDATION	300.00	495.00
DISBURSEMENT TANKS	295.00	790.00
SPRAY WATERPROOFING	105.00	895.00
		-
		-
		-
		-
		-
TOTAL	$ 895.00	

SAMPLE

FIGURE 10-3
(Continued)

ITEMIZED COST DETAIL FORM

EXTERIOR MASONRY / SIDING / GUTTERS:	AMOUNT	SUBTOTALS
MASONRY	12,500.00	
STONE MASONRY	5,000.00	17,500.00
DRYVIT / STUCCO	5,000.00	22,500.00
SIDING	7,000.00	29,500.00
GUTTERS	700.00	30,200.00
SOFFITS	400.00	30,600.00
SIDING INSTALLATION LABOR	2,000.00	32,600.00
GUTTER INSTALLATION LABOR		
		-
		-
		-
		-
		-
TOTAL	$ 32,600.00	

STEEL / IRON:	AMOUNT	SUBTOTALS
STEEL / IRON - DRIVEWAY	200.00	
STEEL / IRON - FOUNDATION	300.00	500.00
STEEL / IRON - INTERIOR	300.00	800.00
		-
		-
		-
		-
		-
TOTAL	$ 800.00	

LUMBER/TRUSSES/FRAMING MATERIALS:	AMOUNT	SUBTOTALS
TRUSSES	8,000.00	
FRAMING LUMBER	11,000.00	19,000.00
SUBFLOOR MATERIALS	3,000.00	22,000.00
MISC. ADHESIVES/NAILS/WRAPS	1,500.00	23,500.00
ROOFING SHEETING	2,500.00	26,000.00
CRANE TO SET TRUSSES	900.00	26,900.00
TOTAL	$ 26,900.00	

SAMPLE

FIGURE 10-3
(*Continued*)

ITEMIZED COST DETAIL FORM

ROOFING MATERIALS & LABOR:	AMOUNT	SUBTOTALS
FELT PAPER	600.00	
SHINGLES / RIDGEVENT	4,800.00	5,400.00
INSTALLATION LABOR	3,500.00	8,900.00
DELIVERY / CRANE	200.00	9,100.00
TOTAL	$ 9,100.00	

WINDOWS AND EXTERIOR DOORS	AMOUNT	SUBTOTALS
WINDOWS	13,000.00	
ENTRANCE DOOR / SIDELIGHTS	3,000.00	16,000.00
ENTRANCE DOOR TRANSOM	1,000.00	17,000.00
REAR DOOR	200.00	17,200.00
SLIDING GLASS DOORS	600.00	17,800.00
GARAGE SERVICE DOOR	200.00	18,000.00
GARAGE DOORS & OPENERS	1,500.00	19,500.00
		-
		-
		-
		-
TOTAL	$ 19,500.00	

PLUMBING MATERIALS / LABOR:	AMOUNT	SUBTOTALS
PLUMBING LABOR	4,000.00	
PLUMBING FIXTURES	7,000.00	11,000.00
		-
TOTAL	$ 11,000.00	

CARPENTRY LABOR:	AMOUNT	SUBTOTALS
FRAMING LABOR	15,000.00	
TRIM CARPENTRY	9,000.00	24,000.00
PROJECT LABOR (CLEAN-UP)	5,000.00	29,000.00
TOTAL	$ 29,000.00	

FIGURE 10-3
(Continued)

ITEMIZED COST DETAIL FORM

ELECTRICAL WIRING / LABOR / FIXTURES:	AMOUNT	SUBTOTALS
ELECTRICAL LABOR / WIRING	5,000.00	
ELECTRICAL FIXTURES:	2,500.00	7,500.00
		-
TOTAL	$ 7,500.00	

INSULATION / DRYWALL / PAINTING:	AMOUNT	SUBTOTALS
INSULATION	3,200.00	
DRYWALL	10,000.00	13,200.00
PAINTING	10,000.00	23,200.00
		-
		-
		-
TOTAL	$ 38,200.00	

MIRRORS / SHELVING/SHOWERDOORS	AMOUNT	SUBTOTALS
MIRRORS	875.00	
SHELVING	1,100.00	1,975.00
SHOWERDOORS	1,000.00	2,975.00
TOWELBARS	300.00	3,275.00
		-
		-
TOTAL	$ 3,275.00	

CABINETS/APPLIANCES/COUNTERTOPS	AMOUNT	SUBTOTALS
CABINETS	15,000.00	
COUNTERTOPS		15,000.00
RANGE	800.00	15,800.00
REFRIGERATOR	1,200.00	17,000.00
MICROWAVE	600.00	17,600.00
OVEN		17,600.00
WASHER / DRYER	1,200.00	18,800.00
		-
		-
		-
		-
TOTAL	$ 18,800.00	

FIGURE 10-3
(*Continued*)

ITEMIZED COST DETAIL FORM

FIREPLACE / MANTLE:	AMOUNT	SUBTOTALS
FIREBOX	2,000.00	
MANTLE	1,200.00	3,200.00
		-
TOTAL	$ 3,200.00	

FINISH FLOORING	AMOUNT	SUBTOTALS
CERAMIC TILE	10,000.00	
LINOLEUM		10,000.00
CARPETING	5,000.00	15,000.00
HARDWOOD / LAMINATE		15,000.00
STONE / SLATE	6,000.00	21,000.00
		-
		-
		-
		-
TOTAL	$ 21,000.00	

CLEANING	AMOUNT	SUBTOTALS
DUMPSTER FEES	1,500.00	
WINDOW CLEANING	600.00	2,100.00
FINAL CONSTRUCTION CLEAN-UP	1,200.00	3,300.00
		-
		-
		-
TOTAL	$ 3,300.00	

LANDSCAPING	AMOUNT	SUBTOTALS
FINISH GRADE	2,500.00	
SOD / SEED	4,500.00	7,000.00
TREES	3,000.00	10,000.00
		-
TOTAL	$ 10,000.00	

FIGURE 10-3
(Continued)

ITEMIZED COST DETAIL FORM

MISC. EXPENSES & RENTALS:	AMOUNT	SUBTOTALS
CRANE RENTAL	200.00	
PORTABLE HEATER RENTAL	75.00	275.00
		-
		-
		-
		-
		-
		-
		-
		-
		-
		-
		-
		-
		-
		-
		-
		-
		-
TOTAL	$ 275.00	

SAMPLE

FIGURE 10-3
(*Continued*)

SAMPLE COST DETAIL FORM

When you have decided on a particular vendor or subcontractor and have accepted his or her bid or estimate, you will record the name of whom you selected in the *subcontractor/vendor* column and the amount of their bid in the *amount of estimate* column. This will be your control column and it is the number you do not want to exceed during construction. You will refer back to this paper often during construction and once a category of construction is complete, you will enter the total from the itemized cost detail form into the *actual cost* column of this form. You will then subtract the actual cost from the amount of estimate to get an overage or balance available. Some areas will be an overage, but some areas will be less than originally thought and leave a balance. The most important number to keep track of is the accumulation of actual costs, and keep that number in comparison with the total amount of estimates. If you see you have numerous overages, you need to scan areas of soft costs to see if you can cut some costs to make up for the overages or discuss your situation with your lender early during construction. There are some circumstances where overages cannot be predicted and are bound to happen. One of the most common is excavation because of running into an unforeseen situation with the property such as extra rock or an underground spring. A lender is usually more accommodating in these situations over a large overage in a soft cost area (Fig. 10-4).

SAMPLE COST DETAIL FORM

LOT NUMBER: <u>123</u> SUBDIVISION: <u>HAPPY ACRES</u>

HOMEOWNER: <u>MR. AND MRS. HAPPY COUPLE</u>

	Item	Subcontractor / Vendor	Amount of Estimate	Actual Cost	Overage / Balance
1	PERMITS AND TAP FEES	MILLER CO/ABC ELEC, ETC.	500.00	350.00	150.00
2	LAYOUT	A-B ENGINEERING	1,000.00	500.00	500.00
3	BLUEPRINTS AND COPIES	#1 HOME DESIGNERS	2,235.00	2,235.00	-
4	EXCAVATING AND ROUGH GRADING	WE DIG-UM EXCAVATING CO	18,500.00		18,500.00
5	BACKFILL AND FINAL GRADE	WE DIG-UM EXCAVATING CO	5,300.00		5,300.00
6	UTILITY INSTALLATION	UTILIZE US UTILITY COMPANY	2,300.00		2,300.00
7	FOUNDATION		12,000.00		12,000.00
8	FLATWORK		7,500.00		7,500.00
9	WATERPROOFING/DRAINTILE	KEEP DRY WATERPROOFING	895.00		895.00
10	MASONRY EXTERIOR	STONES & BRICKS CO	22,500.00		22,500.00
11	SEPTIC / SEWER SYSTEM	S & S SEPTIC SERVICES	6,500.00		6,500.00
12	STEEL AND IRON	STEEL AND MORE COMPANY	800.00		800.00
13	CARPENTRY LABOR FRAMING & DECK	PLUMB, LEVEL, SQUARE CO	15,000.00		15,000.00
14	LUMBER	WOODY'S LUMBER CO	18,000.00		18,000.00
15	TRUSSES & CRANE FOR SETTING TRUSSES	WOODY'S LUMBER/BIG CRANE	8,900.00		8,900.00
16	WINDOWS / EXTERIOR DOORS	WOODY'S LUMBER CO	18,000.00		18,000.00
17	ROOFING MATERIALS	WOODY'S LUMBER CO	5,600.00		5,600.00
18	ROOFING LABOR	A SHINGLE CO	3,500.00		3,500.00
19	EXTERIOR SIDING	EXCITING SIDING CO	7,000.00		7,000.00
20	GUTTERS / SOFFITS	EXCITING SIDING CO	1,100.00		1,100.00
21	SIDING INSTALLATION	EXCITING SIDING CO	2,000.00		2,000.00
22	MILLWORK / INTERIOR TRIM				7,500.00
23	INTERIOR STAIR PARTS & HARDWARE				2,500.00
24	MISC. MATERIALS/RENTALS				2,500.00
25	PLUMBING LABOR				4,000.00
26	PLUMBING FIXTURES				7,000.00
27	ELECTRIC WIRING	ZZZZT ELECTRIC, INC.	5,000.00		5,000.00
28	HEATING AND AIR CONDITIONING	ALL TEMPERATURE H/AC CO.	7,500.00		7,500.00
29	INSULATION	THERMAL STUFF, INC.	3,200.00		3,200.00
30	DRYWALL MATERIALS/HANGING/TAPING	BIG JIM'S DRYWALL, INC.	10,000.00		10,000.00
31	PAINTING	BIG JIM'S DRYWALL, INC.	10,000.00		10,000.00
32	EXTERIOR DECK MATERIALS	WOODY'S LUMBER CO	7,500.00		7,500.00
33	EXTERIOR DECK MATERIALS - RAILING	THE IRON MATADOR, INC.	5,500.00		5,500.00
34	BATHROOM MARBLE	SINKS AND MORE COMPANY	2,500.00		2,500.00
35	MIRRORS / SHOWERDOORS	REFLECTIONS IN THE DOOR CO	1,875.00		1,875.00
36	SHELVING	PUT IT ON THE SHELF, INC.	1,100.00		1,100.00
37	GARAGE DOORS	QUITE A DOOR COMPANY	1,500.00		1,500.00
38	TRIM CARPENTRY	INTERIOR CONSTRUCTION	9,000.00		9,000.00
39	PROJECT LABOR	A-Z CONSTRUCTION, INC.	5,000.00		5,000.00
40	JOB SUPERVISION / GEN. CONTRACTOR	A-Z CONSTRUCTION, INC.	45,000.00	7,500.00	37,500.00
41	CABINETS AND KITCHEN COUNTERTOPS	KITCHENS PLUS COMPANY	15,000.00		15,000.00
42	APPLIANCES	APPLIANCES USA	3,800.00		3,800.00
43	ELECTRIC FIXTURES	LIGHTS ON THE WALL, INC.	2,500.00		2,500.00

Callouts:
- Line Item Number
- Description of item being furnished.
- Actual cost of materials or services. This may differ from original estimates.
- Amount of bid or estimate for materials or services.
- Specific subcontractor or vendor being used.
- Remaining balance after accrued cost deducted from estimate. If cost is more than bid, this will be a negative number indicating an overage. If the cost is less than bid, there will be a balance remaining. Any balance remaining can be applied to an overage in another area.

SAMPLE

FIGURE 10-4
Sample cost detail form.

SAMPLE COST DETAIL FORM

LOT NUMBER: <u>123</u> SUBDIVISION: <u>HAPPY ACRES</u>
HOMEOWNER: <u>MR. AND MRS. HAPPY COUPLE</u>

	Item	Subcontractor / Vendor	Amount of Estimate	Actual Cost	Overage / Balance
44	FIREPLACE	LIGHTS ON THE WALL, INC.	3,200.00		3,200.00
45	FINISH FLOORING	FLOORS AND MORE FLOORS	21,000.00		21,000.00
46	FINAL CONSTRUCTION CLEAN	A-Z CONSTRUCTION, INC.	1,200.00		1,200.00
47	TRASH / DUMPSER FEE	SUCH A WASTE, INC.	1,500.00		1,500.00
48	WINDOW CLEANING	I CAN SEE CLEARLY NOW, INC.	600.00		600.00
49	LANDSCAPING	GROOM AND GROW NURSERY	10,000.00		10,000.00
50					-
51					-
52					-
53					-
54					-
55					-
56					-
57					-
58					-
59					-
60					-
61					-
62					-
63					-
64					-
65					-
66					-
67					-
68					-
69					-
70					
	TOTAL		$356,105.00	$10,585.00	$345,520.00
	TOTAL SQ. FT OF LIVING AREA		3,500		
	COST / SQ. FT. LIVING AREA		$101.74		

Callouts:
- By dividing the total of Actual Costs by the number of square feet of living area the cost per square foot is determined.
- Total of bids and estimates.
- Accumulation of total actual expenses and total cost of construction.
- Balance of remaining funds.
- Total square feet of living area.

FIGURE 10-4
(*Continued*)

11

Creating Your Construction Schedule

Creating a construction schedule is the key to keeping control of your project. By getting an idea of how long each trade will take to complete, it is easier to move something that has already been scheduled than it is to first get it on the books. Once you establish a rapport with your subcontractors, it will be easier for them to work with you and try to meet your needs.

In the beginning, be sure to ask and note how long it will take to get permits and how far in advance you must call to schedule any inspections. When you are getting the bids from each subcontractor and vendor, be sure to ask how long it will take for them to complete the work or get the product you need. Once you accept a bid or an estimate from a vendor or a subcontractor, note on the bid how long it will take for them to complete their work. This is important and they need to agree to this in any contract you sign with them. They also need to agree that once their crew begins your job, they will not leave your job until it is either completely finished or is as far as they can go until whatever else needs to be completed. Once you get to a point where people are standing around waiting, the subcontractor will start losing money and will pull the crew for another job. Then it becomes difficult to get them back until they are either finished with the other job or to a point where they can stop. This is the place where most builders and homeowners get into big trouble and lose time, which becomes quite costly.

What you don't want to happen is for a subcontractor to give you a great bid, but he is extremely busy and cannot give you a full crew for a full day. In that case, he may give you one man for 1or 2 hours at a time. A job that is slated to take 1 week could take 3 or 4 weeks. This could cause every other subcontractor major problems while they wait for something to be completed before they can start their part of the project.

Example: The insulator cannot start until the plumber, electrician, and heating ventilation and air conditioning subcontractors are finished and any inspections are passed. The electrician has begun pulling wires and installing boxes. He indicated it would be a three-day job. On the second day, the worker leaves a couple of hours early and doesn't show up on the third day. On the fourth day, now one day beyond the schedule, the worker is there for 2 hours instead of 8 hours and is still not finished. On the fifth day he still is not finished because he has begun other jobs and cannot leave them yet. You are now waiting for a few hours of work to be completed so that you can order and schedule inspections. In essence, one day costs you at least a week and quite possibly more than that. This is why it is so important to have your subcontractors commit, as much as is humanly possible, to get their part completed in a timely manner. Be advised, they probably will not sign a contract guaranteeing a specified time schedule. Unless you are a huge builder with extreme clout, the best you can hope for is a sincere attempt to meet some kind of realistic schedule.

When getting estimates and bids for materials, ask how long it will take to get the product. In some cases, windows and doors take a minimum of 21 days or longer from order to delivery, so these items must be ordered as soon as the excavation begins. If ordering specialty items, it may take 6 to 8 weeks or longer for delivery. This is crucial with items such as cabinets. You must take this into consideration when preparing your schedule and notate when the order must be placed. Also check with the vendor because some manufacturers stop production during holiday periods or other times of the year. Trim-out cannot be completed until cabinets are installed. The plumber and electricians cannot finish until the countertops, sinks, and appliances are installed.

Weather is the most unpredictable factor in scheduling. Take this into consideration for determining the best season and month to begin construction. If you are building in an area of the country you are not familiar with, take some extra time to research the climate characteristics of the area. You cannot control the weather, but logistically, if April is the rainy season, you may want to schedule excavation and foundation work to be completed before or after April. Once the house is framed and under roof, weather will have less effect on the construction process. The most important thing is to get under roof as soon as possible so that materials do not get damaged by weather.

When you are getting bids, be sure to ask how far in advance the subcontractors and vendors need to be called for scheduling. If you should encounter a delay or get ahead of schedule, be sure to contact everyone affected so they can adjust their schedules accordingly. Most subcontractors should be contacted two weeks before you need them and again one week prior to their scheduled start date, and finally two days prior to their scheduled start date.

The schedule is a guideline for your project. It will help you not only to see how long it will take until you can move in, it will also help budget as to how much interest you will have to pay during the construction process (Fig. 11-1).

SAMPLE CONSTRUCTION SCHEDULE

Item	Description	Called	Scheduled	Projected Days	Actual Days	Days Needed To Complete According to Bid	
1	Get Permits	6/1	6/3				
2	Plot Plan & Stake-Out	6/4	6/5				Releases for Start
3	Order Temporary Power -	6/1	6/3	2	3	2	Permits
4	Order Trusses and Any Metal or Wood Beams						
5	Order Windows						
6	Order Exterior Doors	6/1	6/22			2	Stake Out
7	Excavation	6/1	6/7				
8	Footings	6/7	6/15			5	Excavation
9	**Inspect: Footings / Steel**	**6/15**	**6/17**				
10	Foundation	6/7	6/20				
11	**Inspect: F**	**6/15**	**6/21**				
12	Waterproof	**6/20**	**6/25**				
13	Flatwork: Basement & Garage	6/17	6/28			2	Sewer Extension
14	Flatwork: Outside	6/17	6/30				
15	Backfill & Rough Grade					2	Waterproofing
16	Lumber						
17	Framing	6/20	7/2			1	Backfill
18	Plumbing Rough	7/2	7/20				
19	HVAC Rough	7/2	7/21				Lumber Delivery
20	Electric Rough	7/2	7/23				
21	Order Interior & Exterior Handrails	7/2	7/23			7	Start Framing
22	Fireplace Box Installation	7/2	7/23				
23	Tub & Shower Installation	6/20	7/15			10	Finish Framing
24	Truss Delivery	7/2					
25	Roof Load Materials	7/2	7/1			3	Roofing
26	Masonry / Dryvit Installation		7/25			2	Rough Plumbing
27	Siding Installation	7/20	7/30			4	Electric / HVAC
28	Gutter & Soffit Installation	7/20	8/5				
29	Insulation	7/25	8/3			2	Insulation
30	Drywall Stock	7/30	8/7				
31	**Inspect: Framing /Plumbing Rough /Electrical Rough**	**7/30**	**8/2**			5	Drywall Hang
32	Garage Door Installation	8/1	8/8				
33	Drywall Hanging	7/25	8/9			9	Drywall Tape/Sand
34	**Inspect: Drywall**	**8/13**	**8/15**				
35	Drywall Taping	8/13	8/16			5	Paint
36	Order Showerdoors and Mirrors	8/13	9/10				
37	Order Marble Tops	8/13	9/10			3	Hang Doors
38	Order Cabinets	8/13	9/10				
39	Interior Paint	8/13	9/1			5	Tile
40	HVAC Final	9/10	9/15				
41	Hang Interior Doors					2	Carpet
42	Shelving Installation						
43	Tile Installation					15	Cabinets / Final Trim
44	Marble Installation						Final
45	Plumbing Final / Install Fi					3	Plumbing/Electric
46	Electric Final / Install Fixtu						
47	Install Electric Meter and					2	Carpenter Final
48	Interior & Exterior Handra						
49	Interior Trim and Rehang D					1	Drywall Touch Up
50	Showerdoor and Mirror Installation	9/15	10/7				
51	Window Clean	10/1	10/10			1	Paint Touch Up
52	Carpet Installation	10/1	10/11				
53	Paint Touch Up	10/7	10/15			1	Windows / Clean
54	Trim Carpenter	9/15	9/30				
55	Construction Clean	10/10	10/17			1	Final Inspection
56	Occupancy Inspection	10/17	10/19				
						1	Walk Through

Callout notes on figure:
- The projected number of days to complete.
- The actual number of days it took to complete.
- The date the vendor or subcontractor was called to schedule for project.
- The date the materials or subcontractor is scheduled to start.
- The number of days needed to complete according to bid.
- This schedule is a sample. When filling out the schedule refer to the time needed to complete a job according to the bid or estimate for that item.
  *Be sure to adjust the schedule if a subcontractor finishes early or is delayed.
  *Don't forget to take weekends and holidays into consideration when filling out the schedule. Always write in pencil so changes can be made easily.

FIGURE 11-1

Sample construction schedule.

12

What You Can Do to Save Money

If you decide that you want to act as your own general contractor, you can save 10 to 25 percent over the cost of the house. If you do it wrong, it can cost 30 percent or more to fix it. If you have some building experience, being your own general contractor can be a challenging and rewarding experience. If you do not have any building experience, and you still want to be a general contractor, hiring a construction superintendent or construction foreman to check the quality during construction is a must. There are numerous times when the homeowner frets about inconsequential matters and is oblivious to major structural issues that arise. You don't always need to hire an engineer, but by hiring a construction superintendent to check the project occasionally, you are doing some quality control.

A major area in which the homeowner can save money is by cleaning the job site regularly and daily, if possible. A subcontractor deserves to come onto a clean job site to perform his or her trade. By having the site ready for the subcontractor, you are saving his or her time, which is saving you time and money. Some subcontractors clean up after themselves, but do not count on it unless it has been specified in their bid. They do not clean up after the subcontractors who worked before them, and they may charge you if they have to. If you clean the job site daily, everyone has a fresh start each day.

Most of the time they are grateful being able to get to work and get the job finished quickly. It is most helpful to supply a trashcan for lunch trash and marked as such.

There is a small savings by purchasing plumbing fixtures directly from the plumbing supplier and avoiding the markup. However, the markup is usually minimal and if parts are missing, you will have to go back to the supplier rather than the plumber. Also, the plumber may not warrant materials he or she did not purchase.

Get all estimates and bids for everything before you break ground. You can seek out additional bids, estimates, and changes if you have not signed any agreements, but never start construction without knowing what to expect for expenses. Do not think you know the cost of an item. Go get the actual cost. Do not bid over the phone. Take the blueprint to the contractor and let him or her look at it and discuss it in detail. If you are using special materials tell everyone even remotely involved in the very beginning.

The homeowner's construction workbook is designed to help you create a realistic budget. You may still have an overage at the end of the project, but it should be a minimal one and one that you may be able to anticipate early on. If you begin early and do the research needed, you will alleviate a great deal of the stress associated with building a house. Remember, it's just a house.

Now, let's get to work.

13

Frequently Asked Questions

How much is building a house going to cost?

This is a complicated question and deserves a detailed answer. While the entire book is devoted to answering this question, Chaps. 6 and 8 will guide you to find the answer that will suit you and your situation.

How much should the house cost in relation to the property it is being built on?

While this answer varies greatly, a general formula can be found in Chap. 8.

Can I make changes after construction begins?

This may seem like a silly question, but of course you can. However, Chap. 9 gives examples of what changes can do to your budget.

Can we add another bathroom in the basement?

This seems like a simple enough question, but again can present problems if construction is too far along. Chapters 7, 8, and 9 have guidelines for helping you make a decision.

Since the basement is finished, can I store my furniture there?

The answer to this question should always be "no." It does not matter that you own the property or house being built. Besides the liability of loss and damage to personal belongings that will be placed on the builder and subcontractors, all trades deserve a place to do their work unobstructed. See Chap. 12 for details.

When can I move in?

See "After Construction" in the following construction workbook.

HOMEOWNER'S CONSTRUCTION WORKBOOK

FOR: _____

LOT NUMBER: _____ / SUBDIVISION: _____

ADDRESS: _____

CITY/STATE: _____

Contents

BEFORE CONSTRUCTION

General Property Information

General Characteristics of the Property

Permits and Tap Fees

Who Needs What

Blueprint Log Sheet

Comparative Cost Estimates

Electrical Fixture Worksheet

Preliminary Construction Estimates Worksheet

DURING CONSTRUCTION

Itemized Cost Detail Worksheet

Actual Cost Detail

Disbursement Request

Waiver of Lien

Construction Schedule

AFTER CONSTRUCTION

Subcontractor List

Homeowner Responsibilities

BEFORE CONSTRUCTION

The following pages are to be used before construction. Compile and research all items on each page to keep them permanently for your files and for any future owners of the house.

This is the information your builder will need and will be helpful in the future for any realtor.

GENERAL PROPERTY INFORMATION

PROPERTY OWNER(S): _____ _____

LOT NUMBER AND SUBDIVISION: _____ _____

911 STREET ADDRESS: _____ _____

CITY / STATE / ZIP CODE: _____ _____

COUNTY: _____ _____

PROPERTY 911 PHONE CONTACT: _____ _____

PROPERTY IDENTIFICATION NUMBER (P.I.N.): _____ _____

ZONING: _____ _____

SPECIAL VARIANCES: _____ _____

SPECIAL RESTRICTIONS: _____ _____

PROPERTY SETBACKS:
_____ _____

SIDE SETBACK FROM PROPERTY LINE: _____ _____

FRONT SETBACK FROM UTILITY EASEMENT: _____ _____

BACKSET FROM PROPERTY LINE: _____ _____

IMPORTANT LOCAL CONTACTS:	*DISTRICT*	NONEMERGENCY *PHONE NUMBER*
FIRE DEPARTMENT:	_____	_____
POLICE DEPARTMENT:	_____	_____
GENERAL SCHOOL DISTRICT:	_____	_____
ELEMENTARY SCHOOL ADDRESS:	_____	_____
MIDDLE SCHOOL ADDRESS:	_____	_____
HIGH SCHOOL ADDRESS:	_____	_____

GENERAL CHARACTERISTICS OF THE PROPERTY

COUNTY: _____   STATE: _____

IS THE PROPERTY WITHIN CITY LIMITS?   Y___ N ___   CITY: _____

IF THE PROPERTY HAS BEEN SURVEYED IS THERE A PLAT?   Y_____ N _____

ARE THE CORNERS MARKED BY SURVEY STAKES?   Y_____ N _____

SURVEYED BY: _____

_____

_____

WHAT UTILITIES ARE ALREADY LOCATED ON THE PROPERTY?

WATER: Y _____ N _____ CITY _____ UTILITY COMPANY _____

PRIVATE WELL _____ SHARED WELL _____ COMMUNITY WELL _____

SEWER SYSTEM: CITY / UTILITY COMPANY: _____

PRIVATE SEPTIC _____ INSTALLED BY: _____

COMMUNITY SEWER / MAINTAINED BY: _____

GAS: NONE ___   PROPANE / SUPPLIER: _____

GAS: NATURAL _____ GAS COMPANY: _____

ELECTRIC: _____ ELECTRIC COMPANY: _____

TELEPHONE: _____ TELEPHONE COMPANY: _____

CABLE OR SATELLITE COMPANY: _____

WASTE PROVIDER: _____

PERMITS AND TAP FEES

What permits are required?	OFFICE/CONTACT	PHONE NUMBER:	COST / FEE
COUNTY:			
CITY / TOWN:			
SUBDIVISION:			
OTHER:			

Tap fees and deposits for service:

ELECTRIC:			
WATER / WATER METER:			
GAS:			
SEWER:			
TELEPHONE:			
CABLE:			
WASTE / REFUSE:			

What inspections are required?	CONTACT / DEPARTMENT	PHONE NUMBER:	N/A
COUNTY:			
CITY / TOWN:			
SUBDIVISION:			
HOMEOWNERS ASSN.:			
HOUSE PLAN / LANDSCAPE:			
CLEARING:			
HOUSE LAYOUT / SETBACKS:			
EXCAVATION:			
FOUNDATION LAYOUT:			
FOOTINGS:			
FOUNDATION WALLS:			
STEEL / IRON:			

PERMITS AND TAP FEES

What inspections are required?	CONTACT / DEPARTMENT	PHONE NUMBER:	N/A
FRAMING:			
FLATWORK:			
ELECTRIC ROUGH:			
PLUMBING ROUGH:			
INSULATION:			
SEPTIC / SEWER:			
DRYWALL:			
PLUMBING FINAL:			
ELECTRIC FINAL:			
OCCUPANCY PERMIT:			
:			
:			
:			
:			
:			
:			
:			
:			
:			
:			
:			
:			
:			

WHO NEEDS WHAT

This is the basic list of who will need what information you either have gathered or will need to gather.

WHO	NEEDS WHAT
THE LENDER	COPY OF PLAT
	ONE SET OF BLUEPRINTS
	PRELIMINARY ESTIMATE
	DISBURSEMENT REQUESTS WITH INVOICES
	ORIGINALS OF LIEN WAIVERS
THE ARCHITECT / DRAFTSMAN	COPY OF PLAT
	ALL COVENANTS AND RESTRICTIONS
	REQUIRED SETBACK FROM PROPERTY LINES
	RECORDED EASEMENTS
SURVEY ENGINEER	COPY OF PLAT AND PROPERTY LOCATION
MUNICIPALITY OR SUBDIVISION FOR PERMIT APPLICATION	COPY OF PLAT
	TWO FULL SETS OF BLUEPRINTS
	COPY OF PLAT WITH HOUSE LAYOUT
	WATER AND SEWER LINE LAYOUT
HOMEOWNER (These will be important to keep for any future resale of property as well.)	COPY OF PLAT WITHOUT HOUSE
	COPY OF PLAT WITH HOUSE, WATER, AND SEWER LAYOUT
	ONE SET OF BLUEPRINTS
	WARRANTY DEED OR DEED OF TRUST
	ALL UTILITY METER BOX NUMBERS
	MOST CURRENT REAL ESTATE TAX RECORD
	ALL COVENANTS AND RESTRICTIONS

BLUEPRINT LOG SHEET

Vendor or Subcontractor	Material or Trade	Phone Number	Blueprint Page	Date Out	Date Returned
	PERMIT				
	PERMIT				
	PERMIT				
	SEPTIC ENGINEER				
	SEPTIC ENGINEER				
	LOT CLEARING				
	LOT CLEARING				
	EXCAVATION				
	EXCAVATION				
	FOUNDATION				
	FOUNDATION				
	FLATWORK				
	FLATWORK				
	LUMBER				
	LUMBER				
	WINDOWS				
	WINDOWS				

BLUEPRINT LOG SHEET

Vendor or Subcontractor	Material or Trade	Phone Number	Blueprint Page	Date Out	Date Returned
	ROOFING				
	ROOFING				
	FRAMING CREW				
	FRAMING CREW				
	INSULATION				
	INSULATION				
	ELECTRICIAN				
	ELECTRICIAN				
	PLUMBER				
	PLUMBER				
	HVAC				
	HVAC				
	SIDING				
	SIDING				
	MASONRY				
	MASONRY				
	GUTTERS				
	GUTTERS				

BLUEPRINT LOG SHEET

Vendor or Subcontractor	Material or Trade	Phone Number	Blueprint Page	Date Out	Date Returned
	FIREPLACE				
	FIREPLACE				
	DRYWALL				
	DRYWALL				
	PAINTING				
	PAINTING				
	CABINETRY				
	CABINETRY				
	FLOORING				
	FLOORING				
	TRIM CARPENTRY				
	TRIM CARPENTRY				
	MILLWORK				
	MILLWORK				

BLUEPRINT LOG SHEET

Vendor or Subcontractor	Material or Trade	Phone Number	Blueprint Page	Date Out	Date Returned
	LANDSCAPE				
	LANDSCAPE				

COMPARATIVE COST ESTIMATES

CABINETRY:

Cabinet Brand / Style	Kitchen Cost	Master Bath Cost	Bath #1 Cost	Bath #2 Cost	Bath #3 Cost	Laundry Cost	Extra	Extra	Total

NOTES:

PLUMBING FIXTURES:

Cabinet Brand / Style	Kitchen Cost	Master Bath Cost	Bath #1 Cost	Bath #2 Cost	Bath #3 Cost	Laundry Cost	Extra	Extra	Total

NOTES:

ELECTRICAL FIXTURE WORKSHEET

ELECTRICAL FIXTURES:

Room or Area	QTY	Brand	Model Number	Unit Cost	Subtotal
EXTERIOR:					
FRONT ENTRANCE DOOR					
GARAGE DOOR(S)					
GARAGE SERVICE DOOR(S)					
MOTION DETECTORS					
PATIO					
SIDEWALK					
LIGHTPOST(S)					
BACK ENTRANCE DOOR(S)					
SLIDING DOOR(S)					
EXTRA					
EXTRA					
INTERIOR:					
KITCHEN:					
SINK					
ISLAND / BAR					
CABINET INDIRECT					
BREAKFAST NOOK					
CEILING					
ENTRY FOYER					
HALLWAY - LOWER LEVEL					
HALLWAY - MAIN LEVEL					
HALLWAY - UPPER LEVEL					
HALLWAY - BASEMENT					
GREATROOM:					
CEILING					
CEILING FAN					
ABOVE FIREPLACE					
CAN LIGHTS					
FORMAL LIVINGROOM					
DINING ROOM					
			SUBTOTAL	PAGE 1	$

ELECTRICAL FIXTURE WORKSHEET

Room or Area	QTY	Brand	Model Number	Unit Cost	Subtotal
SITTING ROOM					
MASTER BEDROOM:					
CEILING					
CEILING FAN					
CAN LIGHTS					
WALL SCONCE					
MASTER CLOSET(S)					
MASTER BATHROOM:					
CAN LIGHTS					
CEILING					
VANITY NUMBER 1					
VANITY NUMBER 2					
BEDROOM NUMBER 1:					
CEILING					
CEILING FAN					
CAN LIGHTS					
BEDROOM NUMBER 2:					
CEILING					
CEILING FAN					
CAN LIGHTS					
BEDROOM NUMBER 3:					
CEILING					
CEILING FAN					
CAN LIGHTS					
DEN / OFFICE:					
CEILING					
CEILING FAN					
BATHROOM NUMBER 1:					
CEILING					
VANITY					
BATHROOM NUMBER 2:					
CEILING					
VANITY					
			SUBTOTAL	**PAGE 2**	$

ELECTRICAL FIXTURE WORKSHEET

Room or Area	QTY	Brand	Model Number	Unit Cost	Subtotal
POWDER ROOM:					
CEILING					
VANITY					
LAUNDRY ROOM:					
STAIRWELL - SECOND STORY					
STAIRWELL - BASEMENT					
BASEMENT:					
CEILING					
CEILING FAN(S)					
CAN LIGHTS					
CLOSET(S):					
ADDITIONAL ROOMS:					
SUBTOTAL PAGE 3					$
SUBTOTAL FROM PAGE 1					
SUBTOTAL FROM PAGE 2					
SUBTOTAL FROM PAGE 3					
ELECTRICAL FIXTURE TOTAL					$

PRELIMINARY CONSTRUCTION ESTIMATES WORKSHEET

LOT NUMBER: _____   **SUBDIVISION:** _____

HOMEOWNER: _____

	Item or Description	Vendor / Subcontractor	Amount of Estimate Number 1	Amount of Estimate Number 2
1	ALL PERMIT FEES			
2	ALL UTILITY TAP FEES			
3	BLUEPRINTS / DRAFTING / COPIES			
4	CLEARING			
5	EXCAVATING AND ROUGH GRADING			
6	BACKFILL AND FINAL GRADE			
7	UTILITY INSTALLATION			
8	FOUNDATION			
9	FLATWORK			
10	WATERPROOFING AND DRAINTILE			
11	MASONRY			
12	SEPTIC / SEWER SYSTEM			
13	STEEL AND IRON			
14	LUMBER			
15	CARPENTRY FRAMING LABOR			
16	DECK MATERIAL AND LABOR			
17	TRUSSES AND CRANE TO SET TRUSSES			
		SUBTOTALS		

PRELIMINARY CONSTRUCTION ESTIMATES WORKSHEET

	Item or Description	Vendor / Subcontractor	Amount of Estimate Number 1	Amount of Estimate Number 2
18	WINDOWS / EXTERIOR DOORS			
19	ROOFING MATERIAL			
20	ROOFING LABOR			
21	SIDING AND LABOR			
22	GUTTERS AND SOFFITS			
23	MILLWORK AND LOCKSETS			
24	TRIM CARPENTRY LABOR			
25	INTERIOR STAIR PARTS / HANDRAILS			
26	PLUMBING MATERIALS / LABOR			
27	BATHROOM MARBLE			
28	ELECTRICAL WIRING / LABOR			
29	ELECTRICAL FIXTURES			
30	HEATING AND AIR CONDITIONING			
31	INSULATION			
32	DRYWALL HANG AND TAPE			
33	PAINTING AND STAINING			
34	MIRRORS/SHOWERDOORS			
	SUBTOTALS			

PRELIMINARY CONSTRUCTION ESTIMATES WORKSHEET

	Item or Description	Vendor / Subcontractor	Amount of Estimate Number 1	Amount of Estimate Number 2
35	SHELVING			
36	GARAGE DOORS AND OPENERS			
37	PROJECT LABOR / JOBSITE CLEANUP			
38	WASTE DISPOSAL FEES			
39	CABINETS / KITCHEN COUNTERTOPS			
40	APPLIANCES			
41	FIREPLACE BOX AND MANTLE			
42	FINISH FLOORING AND LABOR			
43	WINDOW CLEANING			
44	FINAL OCCUPANCY CLEANING			
45	LANDSCAPING			
46	JOB SUPERVISION/PROJECT MANAGER			
47				
48				
49				
50				
		SUBTOTALS		
		TOTAL		
		TOTAL sq. ft. of Living Area		
		**COST PER SQ. FT.		

** Divide the total square foot of the living area into the total cost of construction to get the cost per square foot of construction.

DURING CONSTRUCTION

Once the loan is activated and all permits are acquired, it is time to begin the project. The forms provided in the workbook will be used throughout the construction process to keep track of expenses, materials, subcontractors, and the construction schedule.

ITEMIZED COST DETAIL WORKSHEET

PERMIT FEES:	AMOUNT	SUBTOTALS
SUB DIVISION		
COUNTY BUILDING		
CITY BUILDING		
FIRE INSPECTION		
WATER		
SEWER / SEPTIC		
TERMITE INSPECTION		
GAS		
PHONE		
CABLE		
ROAD / STREET		
ELECTRIC TAP FEE		
ADDITIONAL FEES:		
TOTAL	$	

BLUEPRINTS:	AMOUNT	SUBTOTALS
ORIGINAL		
COPIES		
CHANGES		
ADDITIONAL FEES:		
TOTAL	$	

SURVEY AND LAYOUT:	AMOUNT	SUBTOTALS
SURVEY		
LAYOUT		
CHANGES		
ADDITIONAL FEES:		
TOTAL	$	

ITEMIZED COST DETAIL WORKSHEET

CLEARING / EXCAVATING:	AMOUNT	SUBTOTALS
CLEARING:		
ROUGH EXCAVATION		
ROUGH GRADING		
BACKFILL		
DIRT REMOVAL / DIRT ADD		
FINAL GRADING		
ADDITIONAL FEES:		
TOTAL	$	

FOOTINGS AND FOUNDATION:	AMOUNT	SUBTOTALS
FOOTINGS		
FOUNDATION WALLS		
RETAINER WALLS		
PIER PADS		
ROCK / FILL		
ADDITIONAL FEES:		
TOTAL	$	

UTILITY INSTALLATION:	AMOUNT	SUBTOTALS
ELECTRIC FROM HOUSE		
GAS FROM HOUSE		
SEWER LINE FROM HOUSE		
WATER FROM HOUSE TO METER		
WATER FROM METER TO MAIN		
ADDITIONAL FEES:		
TOTAL	$	

DRIVEWAY AND FLATWORK:	AMOUNT	SUBTOTALS
GARAGE FLOOR		
BASEMENT FLOOR		
SLAB		
DRIVEWAY		
PATIO PAD AND SIDEWALKS		
ADDITIONAL FEES:		
TOTAL	$	

ITEMIZED COST DETAIL WORKSHEET

SEPTIC / SEWER INSTALLATION:	AMOUNT	SUBTOTALS
SOILS ANALYSIS		
SEPTIC ENGINEERING		
SEPTIC EXCAVATION		
SEPTIC INSTALLATION		
ELECTRIC TO PUMP METER BOX		
ADDITIONAL FEES:		
TOTAL	$	

WATERPROOFING / DRAINTILE:	AMOUNT	SUBTOTALS
DRAINTILE MATERIAL		
DRAIN PIPE AROUND FOUNDATION		
DISBURSEMENT TANKS		
SPRAY-ON DAMPROOF SEALER		
ADDITIONAL FEES:		
TOTAL	$	

EXTERIOR MASONRY / SIDING / GUTTERS:	AMOUNT	SUBTOTALS
MASONRY		
STONE MASONRY		
EIFS / STUCCO		
SIDING MATERIAL AND LABOR		
GUTTERS MATERIAL AND LABOR		
SOFFITS MATERIAL AND LABOR		
ADDITIONAL FEES:		
TOTAL	$	

STEEL / IRON:	AMOUNT	SUBTOTALS
STEEL / IRON - DRIVEWAY		
STEEL / IRON - FOUNDATION		
STEEL / IRON - INTERIOR		
ADDITIONAL FEES:		
TOTAL	$	

ITEMIZED COST DETAIL WORKSHEET

LUMBER / TRUSSES / FRAMING MATERIALS:	AMOUNT	SUBTOTALS
TRUSSES / TRUSS MATERIAL		
FRAMING LUMBER		
SUBFLOOR MATERIALS		
MISCELLANEOUS ADHESIVES/NAILS/WRAPS		
ROOF SHEETING		
CRANE TO SET TRUSSES		
ADDITIONAL FEES:		
TOTAL	$	

ROOFING MATERIALS AND LABOR:	AMOUNT	SUBTOTALS
FELT PAPER		
SHINGLES / RIDGE VENT		
INSTALLATION LABOR		
DELIVERY / CRANE		
ADDITIONAL FEES:		
TOTAL	$	

WINDOWS AND EXTERIOR DOORS:	AMOUNT	SUBTOTALS
WINDOWS		
ENTRANCE DOOR / SIDELIGHTS		
ENTRANCE DOOR TRANSOM		
SLIDING GLASS / FRENCH DOORS		
GARAGE SERVICE DOOR(S)		
REAR ENTRY DOORS		
GARAGE DOOR(S) AND OPENERS		
ADDITIONAL FEES:		
TOTAL	$	

PLUMBING MATERIALS / LABOR:	AMOUNT	SUBTOTALS
PLUMBING FIXTURES		
PLUMBING LABOR		
ADDITIONAL FEES:		
TOTAL	$	

ITEMIZED COST DETAIL WORKSHEET

CARPENTRY LABOR:	**AMOUNT**	**SUBTOTALS**
FRAMING LABOR		
DECK LABOR		
TRIM-OUT CARPENTRY		
PROJECT LABOR (JOB SITE CLEANUP)		
ADDITIONAL FEES:		
TOTAL	$	

ELECTRICAL WIRING/LABOR/FIXTURES:	**AMOUNT**	**SUBTOTALS**
ELECTRICAL WIRING AND LABOR		
ELECTRICAL FIXTURES		
ADDITIONAL FEES:		
TOTAL	$	

INSULATION / DRYWALL / PAINTING:	**AMOUNT**	**SUBTOTALS**
INSULATION		
DRYWALL HANG AND TAPE		
PAINTING / STAINING		
DECK SEALING		
ADDITIONAL FEES:		
TOTAL	$	

MIRRORS/SHELVING/SHOWER DOORS:	**AMOUNT**	**SUBTOTALS**
MIRRORS		
SHELVING		
SHOWER DOORS		
TOWEL BARS		
ADDITIONAL FEES:		
TOTAL	$	

FIREPLACE AND MANTEL:	**AMOUNT**	**SUBTOTALS**
FIREBOX		
MANTLE		
ADDITIONAL FEES:		
TOTAL	$	

ITEMIZED COST DETAIL WORKSHEET

CABINETS/APPLIANCES/COUNTERTOPS:	AMOUNT	SUBTOTALS
CABINETS		
COUNTERTOPS		
RANGE / STOVE		
REFRIGERATOR		
MICROWAVE		
DISHWASHER		
OVEN		
WASHER / DRYER		
ADDITIONAL FEES:		
TOTAL	$	

FINISH FLOORING:	AMOUNT	SUBTOTALS
CERAMIC TILE		
WALL TILE - KITCHEN / BATH		
LINOLEUM		
CARPETING		
HARDWOOD / LAMINATE		
STONE / SLATE		
ADDITIONAL FEES:		
TOTAL	$	

CLEANING:	AMOUNT	SUBTOTALS
DUMPSTER FEES		
WINDOW CLEANING		
FINAL CONSTRUCTION CLEANUP		
FINAL CLEANING PRIOR TO OCCUPANCY		
ADDITIONAL FEES:		
TOTAL	$	

LANDSCAPING:	AMOUNT	SUBTOTALS
FINISH GRADE		
SOD / SEED		
TREES / SHRUBS / FLOWERS		
ADDITIONAL FEES:		
TOTAL	$	

ITEMIZED COST DETAIL WORKSHEET

MISCELLANEOUS EXPENSES AND RENTALS:	AMOUNT	SUBTOTALS
_____	_____	_____
_____	_____	_____
_____	_____	_____
_____	_____	_____
_____	_____	_____
_____	_____	_____
_____	_____	_____
_____	_____	_____
_____	_____	_____
_____	_____	_____
_____	_____	_____
_____	_____	_____
_____	_____	_____
_____	_____	_____
_____	_____	_____
_____	_____	_____
_____	_____	_____
_____	_____	_____
_____	_____	_____
_____	_____	_____
_____	_____	_____
_____	_____	_____
_____	_____	_____
_____	_____	_____
_____	_____	_____
_____	_____	_____
_____	_____	_____
_____	_____	_____
_____	_____	_____
TOTAL	$	_____

ACTUAL COST DETAIL

LOT NUMBER: _____ SUBDIVISION: _____

HOMEOWNER: _____

	Item	Subcontractor / Vendor	Amount of Estimate	Actual Cost
1	PERMITS			
2	UTILITY TAP FEES			
3	SURVEYING AND ENGINEERING			
4	BLUEPRINTS AND COPIES			
5	CLEARING			
6	EXCAVATING AND ROUGH GRADING			
7	BACKFILL AND FINAL GRADE			
8	UTILITY INSTALLATION			
9	FOUNDATION			
10	FLATWORK			
11	WATERPROOFING / DRAINTILE			
12	SEWER / SEPTIC SYSTEM			
13	STEEL AND IRON			
14	LUMBER			
15	TRUSSES AND CRANE TO SET			
16	WINDOWS / EXTERIOR DOORS			
17	CARPENTRY FRAMING LABOR			
18	ROOFING MATERIAL AND LABOR			
19	MASONRY (INTERIOR AND EXTERIOR)			
20	SIDING MATERIALS AND LABOR			
21	GUTTERS AND SOFFITS			
22	INSULATION			
23	ELECTRIC WIRING AND LABOR			
24	PLUMBING MATERIALS AND LABOR			
25	HVAC			
26	DRYWALL HANG AND TAPE			
27	PAINTING MATERIAL AND LABOR			
28	EXTERIOR DECK MATERIALS AND LABOR			
29	MILLWORK / LOCKSETS			
30	INTERIOR STAIR MATERIALS			

ACTUAL COST DETAIL

LOT NUMBER: _____ SUBDIVISION: _____

HOMEOWNER: _____

	Item	Subcontractor / Vendor	Amount of Estimate	Actual Cost
31	TRIM CARPENTRY			
32	FIREPLACE BOX AND MANTEL			
33	MISC. MATERIALS AND RENTALS			
34	PROJECT CLEANUP AND WASTE REMOVAL			
35	BATHROOM MARBLE			
36	ELECTRIC FIXTURES			
37	CABINETS AND COUNTERTOPS			
38	MIRRORS AND SHOWER DOORS			
39	SHELVING			
40	APPLIANCES			
41	FINISH FLOORING			
42	LANDSCAPING			
43	WINDOW CLEANING			
44	PROJECT SUPERVISION AND MANAGEMENT			
45	OCCUPANCY CLEANING			
46				
47				
48				
49				
50				
51				
52				
53				
54				
55				
		TOTALS		
		TOTAL SQ. FT. OF LIVING AREA		
	DIVIDE TOTAL SQ. FT. INTO *ACTUAL* TOTAL TO GET THE TOTAL COST / SQ. FT.			

DISBURSEMENT REQUEST

LOT NUMBER: _____ SUBDIVISION: _____

HOMEOWNER/BORROWER: _____

Subcontractor or Vendor	LIEN WVR Y/N	Description or Services Rendered	Detail Item Number	Check Number Issued	Payment Amount

TOTAL PAYOUT $ _____

NOTE:

We the undersigned certify that this disbursement request for payout is based on work in progress and/or materials furnished for the building project as identified above.

TOTAL REQUESTED FROM LENDER $ _____

SIGNED: _____   DATE: _____
HOMEOWNER / BORROWER

SIGNED: _____   DATE: _____
PROJECT MANAGER

DRAW NUMBER: _____

WAIVER OF LIEN

State of: _____

County of: _____

To All Whom It May Concern:

Whereas, the undersigned has been employed by:

_____

to furnish labor and/or materials for the building known as:

LOT NUMBER: _____ **SUBDIVISION:** _____

ADDRESS: _____

Now, therefore, the undersigned for and in consideration of the sum of ($_____)

_____

good and valuable considerations, the receipt whereof is hereby acknowledged, does hereby waive and release any and all lien, and claim or right to lien, on said above described building and real estate under the Statutes of the State of _____ relating to Mechanic's Liens, on account of Labor or Materials, or both, here to fore furnished by the undersigned for said building and real estate.

In the event the bank check given in payment of the foregoing materials and/or labor should be returned unpaid because of any fault or neglect of the make of the check, then this release shall become null and void.

Given under our hands this _____ day of _____, 20___.

By: _____

Title: _____

Company: _____

Invoice Number: _____

Check Number: _____

CONSTRUCTION SCHEDULE

LOT NUMBER: _____

SUBDIVISION: _____

Item	Description	Called	Scheduled	Projected Days	Actual Days	Days Needed To Complete According to Bid
1	Get Permits					
2	Plot Plan and Stake Out					Releases for Start Permits
3	Order Temporary Power -					
4	Order Trusses and Any Metal or Wood Beams					
5	Order Windows					Lumber Set-Up
6	Order Exterior Doors					
7	Excavation					Stake Out
8	Footings					
9	**Inspect: Footings / Steel**					Excavation
10	Foundation / Metal or Wood Beams					
11	**Inspect: Foundation / Termite**					Footing / Foundation
12	Waterproofing / Draintile					
13	Flatwork: Basement & Garage					Sewer Extension
14	Flatwork: Outside					
15	Backfill and Rough Grade					Waterproofing
16	Lumber					
17	Framing					Backfill
18	Plumbing Rough					
19	HVAC Rough					Lumber Delivery
20	Electric Rough					
21	Order Interior and Exterior Handrails					Start Framing
22	Fireplace Box Installation					
23	Tub & Shower Installation					Finish Framing
24	Truss Delivery					
25	Roof Load Materials					Roofing
26	Masonry / Dryvit Installation					Rough Plumbing
27	Siding Installation					Electric / HVAC
28	Gutter and Soffit Installation					
29	Insulation					Insulation
30	Drywall Stock					
31	**Inspect: Framing /Plumbing Rough /Electrical Rough**					Drywall Hang
32	Garage Door Installation					
33	Drywall Hanging					Drywall Tape/Sand
34	**Inspect: Drywall**					
35	Drywall Taping					Paint
36	Order Shower Doors and Mirrors					
37	Order Marble Tops					Hang Doors
38	Order Cabinets					
39	Interior Paint					Tile
40	HVAC Final					
41	Hang Interior Doors					Carpet
42	Shelving Installation					
43	Tile Installation					Cabinets / Final Trim
44	Marble Installation					Final
45	Plumbing Final / Install Fixtures					Plumbing/Electric
46	Electric Final / Install Fixtures					
47	Install Electric Meter and Permanent Service					Carpenter Final
48	Interior and Exterior Handrail Installation					
49	Interior Trim and Rehang Doors					Drywall Touchup
50	Shower Door and Mirror Installation					
51	Window Clean					Paint Touchup
52	Carpet Installation					
53	Paint Touchup					Windows / Clean
54	Trim Carpenter					
55	Construction Clean					Final Inspection
56	Occupancy Inspection					Walk through

AFTER CONSTRUCTION

When the final nail has been hammered and mirror polished, you have finished. It is good to keep a record of the subcontractors and vendors who worked on your house and how to contact them in case warranty work needs to be done or you have questions once you are living in the house.

Once everyone is finished, it is time to move in. The worst thing anyone can do is to move in before everyone is completely finished. If you move in before everyone is finished, the cost is greater than what can be anticipated. Furniture and boxes are not only a liability, but also a hindrance for anyone who must finish. No one wants to work in a new house what has someone's personal belongings because of possible damage and accusations of theft. Personal belongings also simply get in the way of workers not only making their job more difficult, but also creating a situation of taking longer to get their work finished.

Simply put, do not move anything in the house under any circumstances until everyone is completely out.

SUBCONTRACTOR LIST

LOT NUMBER: _____ **SUBDIVISION:** _____

HOMEOWNER: _____

Subcontractor	Description	Phone Number	Cell Number	Fax Number
	PROJECT MANAGER			
	BLUEPRINTS			
	SURVEYING ENGINEER			
	CLEARING			
	EXCAVATION			
	SEPTIC / SEWER			
	UTILITIES			
	WATER LINE INSTALL			
	FOUNDATION			
	WATERPROOFING			
	MASONRY			
	SIDING			
	GUTTERS / SOFFITS			
	LUMBER			
	WINDOWS			
	TRUSS COMPANY			
	FRAMING CREW			
	ROOFING MATERIAL			
	ROOFING LABOR			
	MILLWORK			
	STAIR PARTS			
	PLUMBER			
	PLUMBING FIXTURES			
	ELECTRICIAN			
	ELECTRIC FIXTURES			
	HVAC			
	INSULATION			

SUBCONTRACTOR LIST

LOT NUMBER: _____ **SUBDIVISION:** _____

HOMEOWNER: _____

Subcontractor	*Description*	*Phone Number*	*Cell Number*	*Fax Number*
	DRYWALL			
	PAINT			
	PAINTING			
	MARBLE			
	MIRRORS			
	SHOWER DOORS			
	SHELVING			
	GARAGE DOORS			
	TRIM CARPENTRY			
	APPLIANCES			
	FIREPLACE			
	FLOORING			
	LANDSCAPING			
	WASTE DISPOSAL			
	CLEANING			
	WINDOW CLEANING			

HOMEOWNER RESPONSIBILITIES

- Keep and fill out all warranty information for all products and appliances.

- Keep a list for callback services the builder will provide for. Ask the builder for details about what is covered by any warranty and what is considered a service call that the homeowner is responsible to pay for. The homeowner should not have to pay for services that pertain to things that were installed incorrectly or incompletely, but will be charged for items that are considered a maintenance issue. For example, a leaky pipe or fitting would be warranted by a plumber for 1 year; however, causing a leak in a pipe because of driving a nail into it would not be covered.

- All lawn maintenance and care of plants is the responsibility of the homeowner. Some suppliers warrant plants for 1 year, but if the homeowner has not properly cared for the plant with water and fertilizer, the warranty is void.

- The homeowner is responsible for maintaining caulked areas including windows, base, showers, and tubs. Once caulking is installed, it becomes the homeowner's responsibility.

- The homeowner is responsible for maintaining decks and exterior wood with paint or protective products.

It is wise to go over your responsibilities with the builder throughout the project and once the construction is finished, are aware of your responsibilities in house maintenance.

Index